Introduction

Places

Culture

Practical Information

△ **Kazimierz Dolny (p78)** One of the most beautiful places in Poland. The town is a confection of Renaissance and Mannerist houses.

▽ **Cracow (p85)** The former capital of Poland, Cracow is still the country's artistic and intellectual centre. The vibrant café society, superb architecture and fascinating history make this one of Poland's most rewarding destinations.

◁ **Wieliczka Salt Mine (p93)** A World Heritage Site, this historic salt mine is staggering, both in its size and for its ornately carved chambers.

△ **Poznań (p71)** Lying at the heart of Poland, this city has long been an important trading centre.

◁ **Masuria (p58)** A stunning landscape dotted with lakes and hills.

△ **Tatra Mountains (p84)** These spectacular peaks in the southeast of the country are a haven for rare wildlife.

△ **Zamość (p79)** This Venetian-designed town has the most perfectly-preserved Renaissance centre outside of Italy, with many beautiful buildings.

◁ **Gdańsk (p42)** This Hanseatic city was the birthplace of the Solidarity movement.

◁ **Malbork (p52)** Previously headquarters of the Teutonic Knights, Malbork is one of the largest fortified sites in Europe.

▷ **Warsaw (p20)** The architecture of the country's capital varies from the painstakingly reconstructed Old Town to Socialist Realism.

Cities, Scenery and Solidarity

Mountains, forests, sandy beaches, culture and history – Poland's got them all and is becoming more popular as a holiday destination. Since the victory of the Solidarity trade union movement transformed life in Poland by throwing open doors to the West, tourists have been embarking on adventures of discovery in a country that has many diverse attractions to offer.

Through a thousand years of dramatic history when Poland was constantly being fought over and divided up by neighbours, the Poles have become masters of reconstruction and renovation. As invaders came and went some left an inheritance of magnificent architecture while others razed towns to the ground. Today there is little evidence of the great destruction the country suffered in World War II, as towns and cities have been masterfully and lovingly restored. Gdańsk, Cracow and Warsaw compete in presenting the most magnificent Old Town.

Although in some parts there is a legacy of pollution left by the old regime, which is now being tackled, there is plenty of unspoilt countryside for nature lovers and those in search of outdoor relaxation. Long, tranquil sandy beaches line the Baltic Sea, and Masuria, the land of a thousand lakes, is teeming with wildlife. The magnificent mountain peaks in the southeast contrast with the widespread lowlands that roll seductively into the dark pine forests. Unusual and original scenery has been preserved in national parks, which also offer a final refuge to many rare species such as the European bison.

VARIETY AND CHOICE

With such a diverse landscape, Poland is a paradise for those who enjoy an active holiday, whether it be hiking, climbing or skiing in the mountains, or fishing, sailing or canoeing in the vast network of lakes and rivers.

Hospitality is a great tradition in this country, characterised by generosity whenever there are

Opposite: the Sigismund Column, Warsaw Old Town
Below: Pieninski National Park
Bottom: traditional Highland dress in Zakopane

guests, and around every corner a warm welcome awaits visitors. Tables groan under the weight of food and this is reflected in the hotels, restaurants and guesthouses that are thriving under private ownership.

The Poles love an excuse for a celebration and the country is steeped in folklore, providing scope for colourful festivals in the summer, when regional costumes are aired. Despite the centuries of foreign rulers, the Poles have held on to their identity and remained patriotic throughout, and revere their famous sons.

Frederic Chopin, born near Warsaw in 1810, spent his adult years away from Poland, but the composer never forgot his homeland in his work, and every year he is honoured in music festivals across the country.

Poland is a bridge between Central and Eastern Europe and visitors will experience a mixture of the unusual and the familiar as they travel. While its infrastructure has not yet reached the standards of the West, with a little patience and understanding almost every situation can be mastered.

Chopin's birthplace, Żelazowa Wola

POSITION AND LANDSCAPE

Although many people still think of Poland as being part of Central Europe, from a geographical point of view the opposite is the case: Poland is situated many hundreds of kilometres west of the geographical centre of Europe, which is actually in Lithuania.

Today the national territory of Poland extends from the Baltic in the north to the Carpathians in the south, from the River Bug in the east to the Odra in the west, covering a total area of 312,683 sq km (120,727 sq miles), which roughly corresponds to the UK and Ireland put together, or half the area of Texas. Poland is bordered by Germany, the Czech Republic, Slovakia, the Ukraine, Belorussia, Lithuania and the Russian Federation (Kaliningrad region), and has a total of exactly 3,538km (2,199 miles) of national border.

Topographically, Poland is primarily flat with two-thirds of the country rising no more than 200m (650ft) above sea level. The numerous lakes found in the north of the country were formed by glaciers during the Ice Age. The adjoining central Polish lowlands are mainly agricultural and the plateaux to the south are the remains of ancient mountain ranges that have been eroded over millions of years. The Carpathian and Sudety mountains form Poland's southern boundary with the highest summit in the country, the Rysy (2,499m/8,199ft), in the Tatra Mountains, the highest range in the Carpathians.

CLIMATE AND WHEN TO VISIT

Poland's climate is classified by meteorologists as 'temperate' – a description frequently disputed by both the country's inhabitants and its visitors. This is because Poland is located in a transitional zone between the milder Western European maritime climate and the harsher Eastern European continental climate, which makes the weather extremely changeable.

The seasons do not necessarily coincide with the calendar either, and can differ considerably from year to year, so that the following description of the country's climate is only an indication of what to expect. Spring is sunny and warm,

Eminent Poles

The lives and achievements of various Poles are detailed in museums, monuments and landmarks across the country. The astronomer Nicolas Copernicus studied in various Polish towns. Marie Curie (née Skłodowska) was born and initially educated in Warsaw. Ludwik Zamenhof devised esperanto. Nobel prize winning authors include Henryk Sienkiewicz, Czesław Miłosz and Wisława Szymborska. Among internationally renowned film directors are Roman Polański, Krzysztof Kieślowski and Andrzej Wada.

A landsacpe in the Świetokrzyskie region

but there are sometimes frosts at night, even in May. In summer, from June to August, temperatures often reach 30°C (86°F); most of the rain falls in the mountains, where thunderstorms are frequent. On the other hand, the weather on the Baltic coast is mainly fine and dry.

In the early autumn, Poland is usually sunny and there is hardly any rain, making this a particularly attractive time of year, especially in the mountains. Winter is not especially harsh in most parts of the country, with temperatures seldom dropping below −10°C (14°F), except in the northeast, where it is colder. In the eastern part of Poland and in the mountains there are heavy snowfalls, providing ample opportunity for winter sports. With its scenery and climate, therefore, this country between the Baltic and the Carpathians has something to offer holidaymakers all the year round.

Below: Śniardwy lake, Masuria
Bottom: tradition in Kampinoski National Park

Economy

In 1989 the new democratic government inherited a rocketing inflation rate, which had reached three figures. Leszek Balcerowicz, a brilliant economist who became finance minister, countered it in 1990 by introducing swingeing price rises and monetarist economic reform. In 1993, with a rise in the Gross National Product of 3 percent, Poland became the first country in the

former Eastern bloc (with the exception of the former German Democratic Republic) to achieve a positive balance of trade figures. Nevertheless, the economy still faces a number of challenges due to a range of historical factors.

Ironically, the Communist-led coalition which gained power in 1993 managed the economy surprisingly well, with annual growth exceeding 6 percent combined with rises in employment, productivity and real incomes. But the old Communist habits of controlling the media and bureaucracy by packing them with party loyalists died hard, and in the 1997 parliamentary elections the nervous voters re-elected a Solidarity-led coalition of about three dozen Christian, conservative and anti-Communist groups. However, these were soon voted out and replaced in 2001 by the Democratic Left Alliance. Lech Kczyński of the Prawo i Sprawiedliworść (Law and Justice) party was elected president of a coalition governemnt in 2005.

Meanwhile, the economy continues to grow. Poland's geographical position allows good access to markets in the East and West, and many raw materials are imported. In fact, Poland is the largest market in Central Europe, with 25 percent of the population under the age of 15 and a well-educated adult workforce.

More than 25 percent of the workforce is employed in agriculture, growing wheat, barley, sugar beet, potatoes and fodder crops. Farming, inefficient by Western standards, has always been undertaken on a small scale and largely in private hands. Small and medium-sized businesses and some of the former state monopolies have been privatised. Much of the euphoria of the initial post-Communist years has evaporated, and the population has discovered that capitalism has its challenges. The big economic question now is what will be the result of Poland's membership of the EU.

GOVERNMENT

The Republic of Poland is a parliamentary democracy. Parliament consists of two houses: the Sejm, the lower house with 460 members, is the highest

Solidarity

The defeat of Communist governments throughout the former Eastern bloc was, in part, a direct consequence of the Solidarity-led opposition to Communism in Poland. Originating in the Gdańsk shipyards on the Baltic Coast, *Solidarność* was a trade union movement formed in 1980. Ironically, the right to form a legally recognised trade union, and the right to strike for improved working conditions, was an initial objective. *(See also box on page 12.)*

Satellite dishes cover an apartment block

legislative body and controls the government; the Senate, the upper house of parliament with 100 members, participates in the legislative process. The national government is the highest body in the land, the next administrative level consists of the 16 political departments into which the country is divided.

The head of state is the president. The first president was the former Solidarity leader, Lech Wałęsa *(see box)*, who was replaced in 1995 by the ex-communist Aleksander Kwaśniewski. The government is led by the prime minister, who commands a majority in the Sejm and who elects a council of ministers.

Establishing a parliamentary democracy after the collapse of communism has been no easy task; the discord between numerous parties and recriminations about the past have frequently resulted in political instability. Despite this, the introduction of electoral reforms has continued the country's political development. This culminated in Poland joining the European Union on May 1, 2004.

Lech Wałęsa
Starting his career at the Lenin Shipyard in Gdańsk as an electrician, Lech Wałęsa could hardly have imagined that he would lead a trade union in 1980, and contest the full might of the Communist regime. As Solidarity became a national opposition movement, it was forced underground when martial law was declared in 1981. Continuing the struggle, Lech Wałęsa was awarded the Nobel Peace Prize in 1983, and became the first democratically elected president in 1990.

NATURE AND THE ENVIRONMENT

Almost a third of Poland is covered by forest, primarily pine, spruce and mixed deciduous and coniferous trees. Botanists have identified thousands of types of plants in Poland, including over 1,200 lichens and almost 1,500 of the more complex species of fungus. In the spring, the fields and meadows are a sea of flowers.

Polish forests are home to numerous rare species that have become extinct in other European countries, such as the brown bear, elk and wolf. In Masuria, visitors are struck by the large numbers of storks that build huge nests on gables and church towers; in spring villages are filled with the sound of their calls.

Poland is a paradise for ornithologists. The Biebrzański National Park in the northeast is a huge marshy area which, in spite, or perhaps precisely because of its inaccessibility, attracts ornithologists from all over the world. In the Woliński National Park on the Baltic coast, for

European bison in Białowieska National Park

example, you can spot one of the very rare European sea eagles, which are the model for the Polish national emblem.

The Białowieski National Park is the oldest forest in the country. It is a protected national park covering 50 sq km (19 sq miles) that extends on either side of the Belorussian border and is home to the last European bison. The rare tarpan, a wild pony, and wild boar are also to be found in this park, which is on UNESCO's World Natural Heritage list and can only be visited accompanied by a guide.

Although Poland is still a popular destination for nature lovers, some parts of the country suffer from environmental pollution. Poland's worst problems are caused by the use of coal and brown coal, the main source of energy, the consequences of which are most evident in the industrial zone of Upper Silesia.

The damage is far-reaching: the acid rain is not only attacking trees and buildings but human health has suffered too; the rate of respiratory illness, cancer and deformities in newborn babies is significantly higher in this region than anywhere else. The country's water has also been affected by over-exploiting natural resources.

While the socialist government avoided environmental problems, they have now become an important public issue. The government has launched investigations into levels of pollution.

Below: a power plant near Katowice
Bottom: Kampinoski National Park

Population

Poland currently has a population of around 38.5 million, 1.8 million of them in the capital and almost all are Poles. While this might seem to be a perfectly normal state of affairs, in the thousand-year history of Poland it is rather the exception. For centuries the country was a multinational state, home not only to Poles but also to its neighbours, to Russians, Belorussians, Ukrainians, Slovakians, Latvians, Lithuanians and Jews as well as to Germans, in particular Prussians and Silesians.

A uniform Polish national state was created only after World War II. This was a painful process for everyone who was then driven out of their homeland, as Poland gained territories which had belonged to Germany before World War II. The Polish inhabitants of large areas of former eastern Poland, however, suffered the same fate at the hands of Stalin. At his instigation, Polish territory was shifted a considerable distance to the west, and whether from Wilno or Lwów, Warsaw or Poznań, after World War II every third Pole was either living in exile or was homeless.

Since Poland's borders were recognised by all parties, relationships between the Poles and the few members of national minorities such as the Ukrainians, Belorussians and in particular the

Below: first communion at Jasna Góra Monastery
Bottom: shopping in Lublin

Germans, who populate villages around Opole, have noticeably improved in recent years.

RELIGION

The Roman Catholic Church pervades all areas of daily life. Western European visitors are constantly surprised at the intensity of the Polish people's faith. However, the position of the Church cannot simply be explained by the deep spirituality of the Polish people, it can only be understood in the context of the country's history.

The Church often assumed the role of the State during periods of foreign occupation, and provided spiritual strength in times of national crisis. This patriarchal position inevitably brought the Church into conflict with the atheistic, socialist government after World War II.

This conflict was one of the factors that contributed to the decline of the Communist system. The intense bond between the Church and the people supported them in the darkest periods of the 20th century. Throughout the occupation by Nazi Germany and the terrors of the Stalinist regime, as well as the persistent endeavours of the Communist leaders to reform Poland, the Church stood firm. In 1976, when the Polish conference of bishops published a pastoral in which the Roman Catholic Church was portrayed as the legitimate representative of the nation, it received the people's unanimous approval. The election of Cardinal Karol Wojtyła as Pope in 1978 (see box) strengthened the position of the church still further. A year later, on his first journey home, the Pope encouraged millions of his countrymen with the words: 'Do not be afraid!'

But without a common opponent, the social significance of the Church has changed. Many practising, believing Catholics are now more likely to question or react against the constant dictates of the Church. Nevertheless, the traditional belief and piety remains an expression of the country's cultural, national and social life. The Catholic Church even has its own national radio station, Radio Maria, based in Toruń.

The Polish Pope

Karol Wojtyła (Pope John Paul II) was born in Wadowice, near Cracow, and his childhood home is now a museum. The first Mass he said, following his ordination, was in the crypt of Cracow's Wawel Cathedral, where he remained for 10 years after being appointed Bishop of Cracow. The study he used during this period has been preserved in Cracow's Archdiocesan Museum. Appointed Pope in 1978 he was buried in the Vatican in 2005.

A wooden shrine in the Podhale region

HISTORICAL HIGHLIGHTS

120,000 years ago The earliest traces of humans come from a cave in the Pradnik River valley in the Cracow-Częstochowa Plateau northeast of Cracow.

Iron Age Wooden buildings and artefacts from the Lusatian culture are the first known Slavic settlement, by Biskupin Lake, dating back 2,500 years.

375 The invasion of the Huns triggers the great migration of nations. Slav tribes settle in what is present-day Poland.

966 The founding of Poland. Mieszko I, a powerful Polian chief living in the Poznań region, is baptised. State boundaries extended to include Silesia and Małopolska (Little Poland).

992 Bolesław I Chrobry (the Brave), the son of Mieszko, whose domain for a time included Lusatia, Bohemia and Kiev, is crowned first king of Poland.

1000 In Gniezno the first Polish bishopric is established. German Emperor Otto III visits the city.

1138 After the death of Bolesław III Krzywousty (the Wry-mouthed), the kingdom is divided among his four sons, leading to prolonged conflicts. Poland loses some of its influence.

1226 Duke Konrad Mazowiecki summons the German Order of Teutonic Knights to help him fight the Prussians.

1241 A Polish army under Henryk Pobożny stops the Mongol advance at Legnica, though Cracow is burnt down.

1309 The Teutonic Knighthood has consolidated its power and rules over a large territory along the Eastern Baltic Sea, including the Hanseatic city of Gdańsk.

1320 Władysław Łokietek, Prince of Sieradz, succeeds in reuniting various Polish territories and is crowned king.

1325 Polish-Lithuanian alliance is formed against the Teutonic Knights.

1333 Kazimierz III Wielki (Casimir the Great) doubles the size of his realm, expanding to the east and transforming Poland into a multinational state.

1364 Founding of Cracow University.

1386 Lithuania and Poland are united through the marriage of Jagiello, Grand Duke of Lithuania, with the Polish queen Jadwiga (d'Anjou). Under the Jagiellon dynasty, the country flourishes both culturally and economically.

1410 Teutonic Knights defeated at the Battle of Grunwald, establishing a more powerful, unified realm.

1466 In the Second Peace of Toruń, The Teutonic Knighthood cedes territory, including Gdańsk, to Poland. The Jagiellons rule from the Black Sea to the Baltic.

1505 At the Imperial Diet of Radom the king grants extensive rights to the nobility. establishing the 'rule of the nobility' as a specific Polish form of government.

1543 Nicolas Copernicus publishes *De revolutionibus orbium Coelestium*, stating that the planets orbited the sun.

1552 The Imperial Diet establishes the right of religious freedom. Poland becomes a haven in the turmoil of the religious wars engulfing Europe.

1564 The Jesuits are invited into the country, heralding the start of the Counter-Reformation.

1569 With the Union of Lublin, Poland and Lithuania are united into a single Commonwealth. Warsaw becomes the seat of the joint parliament, the Sejm.

1573–1791 The period of 'elected kings', when the succession is based not on inheritance but election by the aristocracy.

1618–48 Thirty Years' War in Europe.

1621 East Prussia falls to the Elector of Brandenburg. The fate of this region is henceforth determined in Berlin.

1655–60 Sweden invades Poland.

1772, 93, 95 Under successive partitions, Poland is broken up and divided among Prussia, Austria and Russia.

1830–1, 1863–4 The November Insurrection and the January Insurrection are the two most important uprisings against Czarist Russia. Both are brutally crushed.

1892 Polish Socialist Party founded.

1918 After the end of World War I, Poland is reborn. Marshall Józef Pilsudski is proclaimed Head of State. The eastern boundary is established through armed conflict.

1920 Poland stops the advance of the Red Army at the Vistula and occupies part of the Ukraine and Lithuania. Gdańsk becomes a 'free city'.

1921 After heavy fighting between Poles and Germans, Upper Silesia is divided at a conference of ambassadors.

1939 On 1 September, German troops invade Poland, triggering World War II; on 17 September the Red Army marches into eastern Poland. The German army quickly defeats the unprepared Polish army and the Nazis subsequently occupy the country; by the end of the war almost 6 million Polish citizens have died.

1945 After the end of World War II new borders are established by the victorious powers at Yalta and Potsdam. The Communists – the Polish United Workers' Party, PZPR – take power.

1955 Founding of the 'Warsaw Pact' with the Soviet Union and other Eastern bloc states.

1981 Political conflict and strikes, spearheaded by the trade union Solidarity, led by Gdańsk shipyard worker Lech Wałęsa. Martial law is proclaimed, Solidarity is prohibited and thousands are arrested.

1989 Government negotiates with Solidarity and holds elections. Tadeusz Mazowiecki becomes prime minister.

1990 Germany recognises the western border of Poland at the Oder/Neisse line. Lech Wałesa wins presidential election.

1993 The remains of exiled war-time leader General Sikorski are flown home. The last of the 60,000 Soviet troops leave. The former Communists defeat Solidarity in parliamentary elections.

1995 Lech Wałęsa replaced as president by Aleksander Kwaśniewski.

1997 Solidarity-led alliance regains power from Communist-led coalition.

1999 Poland joins NATO.

2001 Democratic Left alliance wins elections and forms coalition government.

2004 Poland joins the European Union.

2005 Pope John Paul II is buried in the Vatican.

Map on page 22

*Preceding pages: the Podhale region and the Tatras
Below: Monument to the Warsaw Uprising
Bottom: the contemporary city*

1: Warsaw

Warsaw (pop. 1.8 million) is a lively, modern metropolis. It is the capital city of Poland, an amalgam of past, present and future, where lovingly preserved historical buildings, stark Communist architecture (Socialist Realism) and the contemporary office buildings of international firms stand side by side.

The inhabitants take great pride in the historic buildings and monuments rebuilt from the devastation of World War II, and strolling through Warsaw's various parks is a popular pastime. The feeling of a new departure after the fall of Communism has been replaced by a new reality, in which some people have succeeded in realising their dreams of a better standard of living, while others have had to face unemployment, and been plunged into poverty by the new system.

HISTORY

In the course of its 700-year history, the city has had more than its fair share of catastrophes, the most brutal of which was World War II. Even the devastation of the 17th-century Swedish invasion, the Tsarist occupation and the insurrections during the partition of Poland, did not leave their mark on the people of Warsaw to anything like the same extent

as the horrors of the last war. Nazi occupation brought years of terror and the obliteration of a large section of the population. Many people were deported to Germany and subjected to forced labour or were sent to concentration camps.

The darkest aspect of the German occupation was undoubtedly that of the Warsaw Ghetto. From 1940, all the Jewish inhabitants, who made up about one third of the population of the city, were crammed into an increasingly diminishing area. Goods trains left daily for the extermination camp Treblinka 100 km (60 miles) away. As the situation for the few people remaining in the ghetto became increasingly hopeless, they resolved to make a final stand: the uprising of the Warsaw Ghetto took place in April 1943. In this desperate battle, the Nazi SS units ruthlessly crushed the rebellion and razed the whole ghetto area to the ground.

The Warsaw Uprising of 1 August 1944, initiated by the exiled government in London, was equally unsuccessful: in 63 days of fierce fighting 200,000 people, most of them civilians, lost their lives either as a result of mass executions or bombings. The Red Army, although already on the outskirts of Warsaw, did not intervene. When it did eventually march in, 85 percent of the city had been systematically destroyed and was virtually deserted. The recently opened **Warsaw Uprising Museum** (Muzeum Powstania Warszawskiego) details this historic rising. Rebuilding began immediately after the end of the war. Visitors to modern-day Warsaw cannot begin to imagine the extent of the devastation.

A tragic heritage

The Warsaw History Museum *(see page 26)* has detailed exhibitions of life under the Nazi regime. This includes a film screened daily showing the methodical destruction of the city by the Nazis, in the three months before they retreated. Hitler ordered the city to be razed to the ground as a 'punishment' for the Warsaw Uprising.

Warsaw Old Town

SIGHTS

Depending on how much time you have, a tour of Warsaw can take a day or last several days. The walk through the Old Town is designed to take up one day. In order to visit the National Museum and the Royal Castle another day is required, and at least one more day is necessary for the excursion to Wilanów. For Wilanów and the site of the former Jewish ghetto, the Palace of Culture and Science and the Łazienki Palace, you will need to take public transport or use your car. The New Town and the

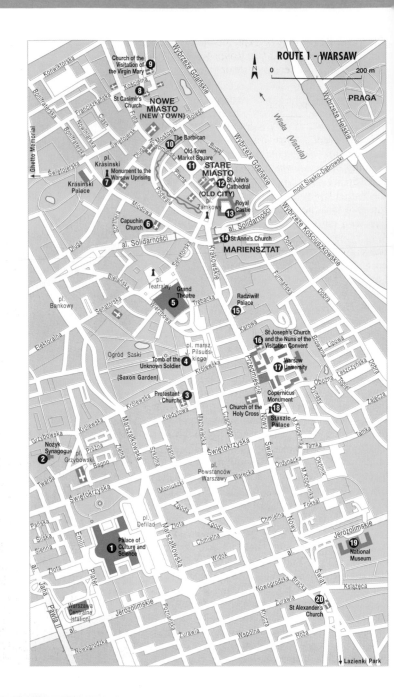

Old Town should only be explored on foot, being largely pedestrianised. The Royal Route (Trakt Królewski) can be seen on foot or by car.

COMMUNIST PALACE

Wherever you are in the city, the massive ★★**Palace of Culture and Science** ❶ (Pałac Kultury i Nauki) is hard to miss. Right in the centre of Warsaw, the building, constructed in 1952–5, is a perfect example of Socialist Realism architecture. A present from the Soviet Union to its Polish 'brothers', it was intended to demonstrate the superiority of Stalinism: with 3,288 rooms on 30 floors, it towers 235m (771ft) into the sky. Today, the capital's Stalinist heirloom is a burden, with immense maintenance costs. Many rooms have acquired new functions, however, and branches of affluent Western companies, gaming halls and offices have established themselves there alongside the more traditional cultural institutions.

Walk north past All Souls Church to the **Nożyk Synagogue** ❷. This rather inconspicuous building, which was restored with the help of American Jews, is hidden behind modern houses and is now the meeting place of Warsaw's few remaining Jews. A few minutes' walk to the east is the **Protestant Church** ❸ (Zbór Ewangelicko-Augsburski), where concerts are regularly held. The neoclassical rotunda, a circular building with a lantern dome dating from 1781, was rebuilt after the war, by contrast with the former Saxon Palace nearby, where all that remains is a fragment of the arcade.

This is now the location of the **Tomb of the Unknown Soldier** ❹ (Grób Nieznanego Żołnierza): at the end of World War I fragments of earth were collected in urns from the battlefields from all over the world where Polish soldiers had fallen. The **changing of the guard** takes place here at noon every day and is one of Warsaw's tourist attractions. Behind the tomb are the ★**Saxon Gardens** (Ogród Saski). With fountains and lakes this is an ideal place for both the local people and footsore tourists to rest for a while from the hustle and bustle of city life and the Warsaw traffic.

Star Attraction
● Palace of Culture and Science

Capital city
Warsaw was proclaimed the capital of Poland in 1596 when King Zygmunt III Waza established a royal residence there. Cracow had been the capital since the early 11th century, after a royal residence was established on Wawel Hill. However, Cracow continued to be the cultural and artistic centre of Poland, with Warsaw the political and commercial centre.

Tomb of the Unknown Soldier

Map on page 22

Jewish Warsaw
The area occupied by the Warsaw Ghetto includes several monuments. On ulica Zamennhofa is the Memorial to the Struggle and Martyrdom of the Jews (Trakt Pamięci Męczeństwa i Walki Żydów) and the Monument to the Heroes of the Ghetto (Pomnik Bonaterów Ghetta). In nearby ulica Stawki is the Umschlagplatz Monument (Pomnik Umschlagplatz) from where Jews were transported to concentration camps.

Krasiński Palace and gardens

MONUMENTS AND PALACES

Walk through the park to the imposing building known as the **Grand Theatre ❺** (Teatr Wielki). This building, with a facade by the Italian architect Antonio Corazzi, is a superb example of neoclassical architecture. With almost 2,000 seats, it is the largest opera house in Poland.

On the opposite side of Theatre Square (Plac Teatralny) is the recently reconstructed facade of the Old Town Hall. Until 1996, the **Monument to the Heroes of Warsaw**, commemorating the fighters and victims of the German occupation of the city from 1939–45, stood on this spot. The monument depicts Nike, the goddess of victory, who, with raised sword, is storming against imaginary attackers. It now stands behind the new building.

The route continues on ulica Senatorska and ulica Miodowa past magnificent former palaces to the baroque **Capuchin Church ❻** (Kościół Capuchynów), dating from the 17th century – in the wall of one of the chapels is the heart of its founder, King Jan III Sobieski – past the **Monument to the Warsaw Uprising ❼** to the baroque ★ **Krasiński Palace** (Pałac Krasińskich). This palace, with an elegant facade, was designed by the Dutch architect Tylman van Gameren in 1677. The building is decorated with two tympana by the young Andreas Schlüter, from the period before he was engaged by the Berlin Court and began his rise to fame. Today the palace houses the **National Library**, which includes a valuable collection of manuscripts.

The palace and the adjoining park are on the western edge of the New Town, which, contrary to its name, is an historic district of the city, neighbouring the Old Town from which it grew, and it is a high point of the city tour.

CONTINUING TO THE NEW TOWN

Those doing the tour by car can make a detour from here to the ★ **Monument to the Heroes of the Ghetto Uprising** in ulica Zamenhofa. It was here that the German leader Willy Brandt knelt in 1970 in remembrance of the victims of the Nazi atrocities. Drivers should look for a parking place near Krasiński Square, since the streets of the historic **New Town** are best explored on foot, and the whole area of the Old Town is in any case a pedestrianised area.

Rising above the New Town Square (Rynek Nowego Miasta) is the dome of **St Casimir's Church ❽** (Kościół Św Kazimierza), a fine building with a Convent of the Nuns of the Holy Sacrament, also the work of Tylman van Gameren, the foremost Baroque architect in Poland. Looking in the direction of the Vistula river (Wisła), is the bell tower of the Gothic **Church of the Visitation of the Virgin Mary ❾**. From the terrace on the east side of the church there is a view across the Vistula to the district of Praga, which lies opposite.

THE OLD TOWN

The ★★★ **Old Town**, established in the 13th century, was reduced to rubble during World War II. Since then it has been completely rebuilt in its original form, using various documents and the highly detailed city views by the 18th-century Italian artist Bernardo Belotto Canaletto, also known as the Polish Canaletto, who was the nephew of Antonio Canale, *the* Canaletto. In its present form, the oldest district of Warsaw is thus a masterpiece

Star Attraction
● Old Town

Below: Monument to the Heroes of the Ghetto
Bottom: in the Old Town

Map on page 22

of Polish restoration work, which has been listed by UNESCO as a World Cultural Heritage site.

BARBICAN

The Barbican ⑩, an impressive structure dating from the 16th century, marks one entry point into the Old Town. Inside and around the Barbican, in fine weather, a wide range of modern art and folk art is offered for sale.

Below: the Barbican
Bottom: Old Town Market Square

The focal point of the Old Town is the **Old Town Market Square ⑪** (Rynek Starego Miasta), which is surrounded by burghers' ornamental houses, dating from the 15th to 19th centuries. It is a favourite meeting place for residents and tourists, who congregate in one of the many cafés and restaurants.

At No. 28, **The Warsaw History Museum** (Muzeum Historyczne Warszawy; open Tues, Thur 11am–6pm, Wed, Fri 10am–3.30pm, Sat– Sun 10.30am–4.30pm; www.mhw.pl) gives a detailed account of the city's dramatic history. Horse-drawn carriages can also be hired here for a scenic tour by those who have had enough of walking.

From the market square, it is only a few minutes' walk, past the Jesuit Church, to **St John's Cathedral ⑫** (Katedra Św Jana), the largest church in the Old Town. Many Polish rulers and dignitaries are buried here, including the Nobel

Prize-winning Polish writer Henryk Sienkiewicz (author of *Quo Vadis*, published in 1896). The Gothic building with impressive star-vaulting dates from the 14th century.

Star Attractions
- **Royal Castle**
- **Royal Route**

ROYAL CASTLE

On the south side of the Old Town is the ★★**Royal Castle** ⓭ (Zamek Królewski; open Tues–Sat 10am–6pm, Sun 11am–6pm; closes 4pm 1 Oct–14 Apr; www.zamak-krolewski.com.pl) where the magnificent interiors have been reconstructed in minute detail. Some of the original furnishings were stored in Canada during the war. It was not until 1971 that rebuilding of the palace was begun, a task that took almost 20 years to complete. In front of the castle is the Castle Square (Plac Zamkowy) with the **Sigismund Column** (Kolumna Zygmunta), a popular photo-stop for visitors to Warsaw. The figure of the king on the column with a huge cross is often taken for a church leader; but it was the Counter-Reformatory zeal of this particular king that inspired the sculptor to put a cross in his hands.

The 'Polish Canaletto'
Among the many impressive galleries and paintings in the Royal Castle, a highlight is the collection of 'Canalettos'. These 22 views of Warsaw and the surrounding area, with their highly detailed architectural nature, give a vivid view of 18th-century Warsaw. They were painted by Bernardo Bellotti Canaletto (1720–80), nephew of the more famous Venetian painter, Antonio Canaletto (Canale).

The Royal Castle and Sigismund Column

THE ROYAL ROUTE

Leaving the Old Town you will find yourself on the ★★**Royal Route** (Trakt Królewski), a series of elegant boulevards connecting the Royal Castle with **Wilanów Palace**. It is lined with prestigious buildings, and some of the city's most historic churches. **St Anne's Church** ⓮ (Kościół Św Anny) is the first building of interest at the beginning of the Royal Route. Originally Gothic, dating from the second half of the 15th century, it was rebuilt a number of times and the present building is in the neoclassical style. The facade is clearly modelled on a church in Venice, Il Redentore, built by the 16th-century Italian architect Andrea Palladio.

Further along, the road widens into Skwer H Hoovera, an elongated square with lawns and flowerbeds surrounding a statue of Poland's greatest romantic poet, Adam Mickiewicz (1789–1855). This monument was erected on the centenary of his birth.

Map on page 22

Equestrian statue of Józef Poniatowski

RADIZIWIŁŁ PALACE

One of the many palaces found along the Royal Route is the **Radziwiłł Palace** ⓑ (Pałac Radziwiłłów), the official residence of the President of Poland. Once owned by the Radziwiłł family, it is also known as the Viceroy's Palace, as in 1819 it was used as the residence of the Viceroy of the Kingdom of Poland. It has been an official state building ever since, witnessing countless official receptions and the signing of important national documents. In the inner courtyard is a statue of the Prince and Marshall of France, Józef Poniatowski, a hero of the Napoleonic war, sculpted by the Danish artist Bertel Thorvaldsen in 1832. The original was destroyed during World War II and the statue that can now be seen was recreated from the replica kept in Copenhagen.

Between former residences of the great families of Poland is the late baroque **St Joseph's Church and the Nuns of the Visitation Convent** ⓰ (Kościół Opieki Św Józefa i Klasztor Wizytek). This has an elaborate facade embellished with columns and a decorative rococo interior. Many consider it to be the most beautiful baroque church in Warsaw.

The boulevard continues to **Warsaw University** ⓱ (Uniwersytet Warszawski). The palaces which once belonged to the Tyszkiewicz and Uruski families and the former Kazimierzowski Royal Palace are now used as centres of research and teaching. Few universities are housed in such beautiful buildings.

FAMOUS POLES

Classical music enthusiasts will want to visit the baroque **Church of the Holy Cross** (Kościół Św Krzyża) diagonally opposite the university grounds: in the left-hand pillar of the main nave is an urn containing the heart of the composer Frederic Chopin, who died in Paris in 1849.

Another renowned Pole, the 16th-century astronomer Nicolas Copernicus *(see page 64)*, is commemorated on the opposite side of the road.

Dating from 1830, the **Copernicus Monument** 🔞 (Pomnik Kopernika, 1830), also designed by Bertel Thorvaldsen, is situated in front of the Staszic Palace, a neoclassical building dating from the 19th century, which now houses the Polish Academy of Science.

At this point a quick coffee break is probably in order, and the Blikle (on Nowy Świat) is just the place. Visitors can relax here and enjoy the elegant period surroundings of Warsaw's most famous café.

This section of the Royal Route extends from Nowy Świat (New World) and it continues into the centre of uptown Warsaw, where the first stop is the ★★**National Museum** 🔞 (Muzeum Narodowe; open Tues–Sun 10am–4pm, until 6pm on Thur; www.mnw.art.pl). Early Christian frescoes from Pharos in Sudan, rescued by Polish archaeologists from the waters of the Aswan Dam, medieval sculptures and examples of Polish painting and decorative art from the past 200 years are highlights of the collection.

A little further south from the National Museum, the tour ends at **St Alexander's Church** 🔞 (Kośćiół Św Aleksandra). This impressive, white neoclassical building, erected in 1818, stands on an island in the middle of Square of the Three Crosses (plac Trzech Krzyży) which also features cafés and boutiques.

Star Attraction
● National Museum

Chopin's birthplace
Approximately 50km (31 miles) from Warsaw in the village of Żelazowa Wola is the beautiful manor house (open Tues–Sun 9.30am–5pm) where Frederic Chopin was born in 1810. With original furnishings and pianos played by Chopin, there are also various mementoes on display. He was baptised in the nearby parish church of Bruchów, where his parents were married.

Inside Chopin's birthplace

Map on page 22

Palace on the Isle

Set in the middle of a lake, complete with swans, and peacocks wandering on the terrace, the exquisite and deeply romantic palace is a combination of neoclassical and baroque. Completed at the end of the 18th century, the palace contains a ballroom, various picture galleries and an exhibition detailing the post-war restoration work, the Nazis having doused the palace with petrol and set it on fire.

The Chopin monument in Łazienki Park

ŁAZIENKI PARK

The bus route (Nos. 116, 122, 193) to ★★ **Łazienki Park** (Park Łazienkowski; open from dawn to dusk daily; www.lazienki-krolewskie.com) follows the Aleje Ujazdowskie, which is a grand avenue lined with buildings comprising a variety of styles. Many of these are embassies, and the office of the prime minister is located here, too. The park, which was opened to the public in 1818, is a haven of peace in the middle of a metropolis.

At the centre of the park is the **Palace on the Isle** (Pałac na Wyspie; open Tues–Sun 9am–4pm), the summer residence of the last king of Poland, Stanisław August Poniatowski, who abdicated in 1795. No one would guess that this magnificent building was originally a bathing pavilion.

The neighbouring **Theatre on the Isle** (Teatr na Wyspie), dating from 1790, was modelled on an ancient amphitheatre. The canal separating the stage from the audience makes it possible to include boats in productions.

The park also has a number of fine neoclassical and romantic buildings, including the Myślewicki Palace (Pałac Myślewicki), and the White House (Biały Domek) which are both museums, the Temple of Diana, and the President of Poland's residence, Belvedere Palace, monuments to the craftsmanship of the architects and landscape gardeners responsible for Łazienki. In the upper part of the park, near the Aleje Ujazdowskie, under a weeping willow, is a statue of Poland's most famous composer Frederic Chopin *(see page 109)* in meditative pose. In the summer, every Sunday at noon an audience of all ages gathers by this Art Nouveau monument to listen to a live concert of Chopin's compositions.

WILANÓW

Take a bus (No. 116 or 180), tram or taxi to reach ★★ **Wilanów Park and Palace** (open Wed–Mon 9am–4pm, until 6pm on Wed and 7pm on Sun 15 May–18 Sept; www.wilanow-palac.art..pl) on the city boundary. The former summer residence of

King Jan III Sobieski, who defeated the Turks in the Battle of Vienna in 1683, is located on the southern edge of Warsaw. Wilanów Palace is considered by many to be the most beautiful secular baroque building in Poland. Set in an extensive park, it has retained all the grandeur of a royal residence. The rooms of the palace were restored after World War II and furnished with the original inventory.

In addition to the historic furniture and valuable porcelain, the famous portraits by Polish artists from the 16th to the 19th century are worth lingering over: look out in particular for the large painting of the early 19th-century owner of the palace, antique collector and archaeologist Stanisław Kostka Potocki, by Jacques-Louis David.

Whether as a mass of blossom in the spring or a shady retreat in the summer, whether golden in the autumn or snow-covered in winter, the Palace Park is enchanting in every season. The gardens, laid out in the English style, extend to a former tributary of the Vistula. Evocatively set among the mature trees are a Japanese bridge, a lake and a Chinese pagoda.

The reputation of the art of Polish posters makes a visit to the **Poster Museum** (Muzeum Plakatu; open Mon 12–3.30pm, Tues– Sun 10am–3.30pm) in the former riding school almost obligatory. The posters are a vivid record of Poland's postwar history and the political role that posters assumed.

Star Attractions
● Łazienki Park
● Wilanów Park and Palace

Below: in the Wilanów gardens
Bottom: a Wilanów Palace sundial

Map below

2: The Baltic Coast

Szczecin – Świnoujście – Kołobrzeg – Słupsk – Gdańsk (652km/408 miles)

If you want to relax on a beach take this route, which extends all the way along the Baltic coast. It is also excellent for families with children. Gdańsk, at the end of the route *(see page 42)*, not only provides a change after the seaside, it is also a must for everyone interested in art, architecture and history. Rebuilt after World War II, Gdańsk is a masterpiece of Polish restoration work and is an essential destination during any visit to Poland.

The starting point of this trip, Szczecin, has also retained much of its original appearance. The route leads through once fashionable resorts such as Kołobrzeg and the scenically beautiful national

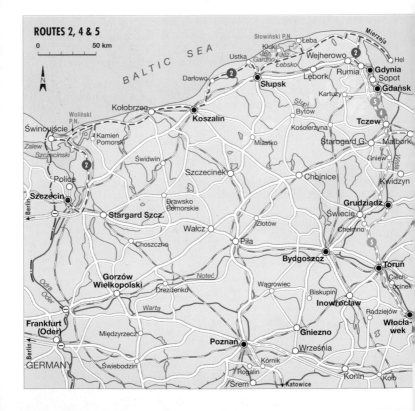

parks, the Woliński and Słowiński are natural habitats for rare species of animals and plants which thrive in these protected environments.

At least seven days are needed to see all the sights, and also have time to relax on the beaches of the Baltic (beaches may be closed due to polluted sea water). Even though the coast has good tourist facilities, it is better to reserve rooms in advance, especially during the holiday season. However, if you are travelling with a tent, your choice of locations will be widened considerably, as there is a plentiful supply of camping and bivouac sites.

Star Attraction
● **Szczecin**

SZCZECIN

The capital of West Pomerania in the northwest part of Poland, ★★ **Szczecin** (pop. 420,000) is a

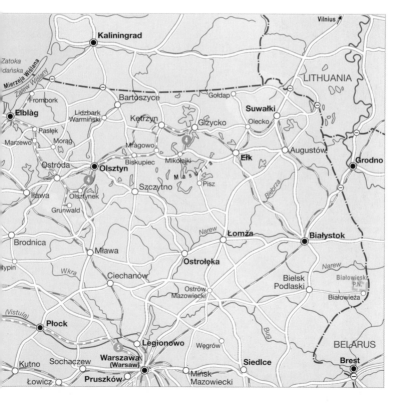

Map below

historic Hanseatic town very close to the German border which, until World War II, was a part of Germany.

WAR DAMAGE

The history of Szczecin, known in German as Stettin, reflects not only its German past, but also the fact that for centuries this harbour town was a bone of contention between Poland, Denmark and Brandenburg, and between the Prussians, French and Swedes. Many fine buildings were damaged or destroyed in the battles between the various factions, but the worst damage was inflicted by the bombing of World War II.

The prestigious buildings of the ★ **Chrobry Embankments ❶** (Wały Chrobrego), which dominate the banks of the River Odra, are one of Szczecin's most striking features. Built early in the 20th century, the buildings include the **Marine Museum** (Muzeum Morskie; open

> **The Hanseatic League**
> The origin of this trading organisation was an agreement between German ports on the Baltic and North Sea coasts, dating from the 12th century. This soon extended to various Polish ports and trading centres, as well as Russian and Scandinavian ports, to total more than 150 towns. The strength of the league began to decline in the 16th century.

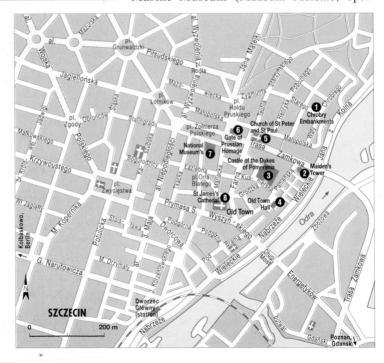

Tues–Fri 10am–5pm, Sat–Sun 10am– 4pm) which has archaeological, ethnographic and maritime collections.

DUCAL SZCZECIN

From here it is only a short distance to the **Maiden's Tower ❷** (Baszta Panieńska), which is also known as the Bastion of the Seven Cloaks, a fortified tower with 4-m (13-ft) thick walls which resisted the bombs of the last war. Above the bastion, looking out over the Odra, is the impressive ★★**Castle of the Dukes of Pomerania ❸** (Zamek Książąt Pomorskich; Tues–Sun 10am–6pm). This residence originally housed the dukes' valuable collection of art treasures; these were later plundered by the Prussians, who converted the rooms into a brewery. Although after 1945 the palace was renovated in the style of a typical 16th-century Renaissance residence, the building still has some of its original Gothic elements.

Only a few paces away from the palace and also on the banks of the Odra is the **Old Town Hall ❹** (Ratusz Staromiejski). After the building went up in flames in 1944, it was rebuilt not in the baroque form that it had acquired in the 17th century, but in its original Gothic form, with the decorative facade typical of north German Hanseatic towns *(see page 41)*. It provides an appropriate setting for the **Museum of the History of Szczecin** (Muzeum Historii Miasta Szczecina; open Tues–Fri 10am–5pm, Sat–Sun 10am–4pm).

The Church of St Peter and St Paul ❺ (Kościół Św Piotra i Pawła) is a fine example of Pomeranian sacral architecture. The brick building, with its complex crow-step gable crowned by a rose window, has retained its Gothic appearance. The church exterior is decorated with glazed terracotta heads and the interior has a fine 18th-century wooden ceiling.

THE HISTORIC CENTRE

In Plac Hołdu Pruskiego is the magnificent **Royal Gate ❻** (Brama Królewska), also known as the

Star Attraction
● **Castle of the Dukes of Pomerania**

Below: ornamental detail on the Castle of the Dukes of Pomerania
Bottom: Szczecin Old Town

Map on pages 32–3

The Polish eagle
The white-tailed sea eagle is an inhabitant of the Wolin National Park, and the Polish national symbol. With a wingspan of 2 metres (6½ feet), this bird of prey lives among various species of protected plants in the forest covering this island – comprised mainly of beech trees – which extends to more than 4,500 hectares (11,120 acres).

Gate of Prussian Homage (Brama Hołdu Pruskiego), a reminder of the sale of the city by the Swedes to the Prussians in 1720. Just a few minutes' walk away from here are several restored 18th-century baroque palaces, one of which houses the **National Museum's ❼** (Muzeum Narodowe; open Tues, Wed, Fri 10am–5pm, Sat–Sun 10am–4pm) collection of medieval sculptures from Eastern Pomerania. In the neighbouring neoclassical **Palace Under the Heads** (Pałac pod Głowami) is a collection of works by contemporary Polish artists.

The largest building in Szczecin is ★ **St James's Cathedral ❽** (Katedra Św Jakuba), a few minutes' walk to the south. This was also no more than a burnt-out ruin after the war, and it was not until 1971 that work began on the restoration of what is one of the largest Gothic churches in Pomerania.

ŚWINOUJŚCIE

Świnoujście (pop. 55,000), 100km (60 miles) away, is of a quite different character. Divided by the River Świna, the two parts connected only by ferry, the town is located on the islands of Uznam and Wolin. This town is the ideal place for those in search of relaxation, with a long tradition as a spa resort. The beach is one of the most beautiful on the Baltic coast and the lighthouse is Poland's tallest.

TREASURE ISLAND

Wolin, one of the three islands which form the estuary delta of the Odra, is popular with animal lovers and above all ornithologists for its large variety of birds. In 1960 most of the island was established as the ★★ **Wolin National Park** (Woliński Park Narodowy). This protected area, which covers 46 sq km (18 sq miles), has provided a stretch of ecologically intact territory for the last white-tailed sea eagles living in the wild, and is also home to many other species of animals.

Well-signposted paths enable visitors to enjoy the scenic beauty of the ancient woods, the numerous turquoise-coloured lakes and the steep cliffs

The cathedral main door, Szczecin

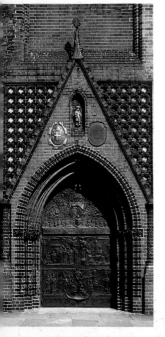

that rise 100m (328ft) high on the Baltic coast. A visit to the **Natural History Museum** (open Tues–Sun 10am–6pm) in Międzyzdroje before setting out will enable you to get the most out of your trip round the park, which includes an animal reserve.

Opposite the island of Wolin on the right-hand bank of the River Dziwnow is **Kamień Pomorski** (pop. 10,000; 153km/96 miles), the historic seat of the Kamien bishops. **St John's Cathedral**, (Katedra Św Jana) originally Romanesque and extended in the Gothic style in the 15th century, is a mecca for music lovers with its 17th century baroque organ. The sound of this instrument in a building with astoundingly good acoustics is enjoyed by organists and audiences every year at the organ festival held in July and August.

A SEASIDE SPA

The next stop is **Kołobrzeg** (pop. 44,000; 226km/140 miles). This spa town, at the mouth of the River Parsęta, owes its existence to salt springs. According to legend, a Pomeranian prince was once hunting in the woods when his faithful dog was attacked by a wild animal. When the hunter cleaned the wound at a nearby spring the dog whined in agony. After the water dried, its fur was white with salt crystals. Whether this story is true or not, it is known that Kołobrzeg was

Star Attraction
● Wolin National Park

*Below: Kołobrzeg lighthouse
Bottom: Wolin National Park*

Map
on pages
32-3

already renowned for its salt deposits as far back as the 9th century.

When the Prussian government put a stop to the salt mining in 1855 for economic reasons, the resourceful citizens of the town exploited the therapeutic value of their salt water springs instead. As a combination of spa and summer resort on the Baltic, Kołobrzeg grew to be Germany's foremost seaside town before World War II, with half a million people visiting every year. The war left its mark here too, though the Old Town district and its buildings of architectural interest have been restored.

The reconstructed ★ **St Mary's Cathedral** (Katedra Mariacka), a red-brick Gothic building that dates from the 14th century, dominates the town with its massive tower. To the right of the church is the neo-Gothic **Town Hall** (Ratusz), designed by Karl Friedrich Schinkel.

The skansen concept

Skansen (open-air) museums can be found throughout Poland, in rural areas or even in a city centre, as in Toruń. Reassembling in a village setting historic country buildings, which represent the region's traditional architectural style, these museums allow you to go back in time and see how people lived and worked, whether in a simple peasant's cottage, a smallholder's dwelling or a mill.

BEYOND KOSZALIN

From Kołobrzeg the route leads through the town of **Koszalin** (pop. 120,000; 269km/167 miles), which includes some 14th- and 15th-century architecture. From here drivers can either take the quick route on the E28 to Słupsk or follow the coast via the picturesque village of ★ **Darłowo**, where there is a romantic Pomeranian Dukes' Castle, and have a refreshing swim at Ustka.

Statue of a fisherman in Darłowo

POMERANIAN HISTORY

★ **Słupsk** (pop. 100,000; 339km/211 miles) is the cultural centre of the region. On the bank of the River Słupia is the Renaissance Pomeranian ★★ **Dukes' Castle** dating from the 16th century and now a museum of the central coastal region. In the Middle Ages the harbour of Słupsk was used to export agricultural products, and the town was famous for its breweries and amber workshops. The notorious **Witches' Tower** (Baszta Czarownic) where, as its name suggests, witches were imprisoned and tortured, dates from the 15th century and is part of the original defensive system which has survived. Słupsk has many other historic buildings, including **St Mary's Church** (Fara Mariacka), with Gothic and Renaissance elements, and the neo-Gothic New Town Hall.

AL FRESCO MUSEUM

On the south bank of Lake Lebsko, surrounded by marshy meadows, pretty woods and reedbeds, is **Kluki** (381km/237 miles), with its Kashubian half-timbered houses. The ★★ **open-air museum** (*skansen*) gives a vivid picture of the lifestyle of the Slovincians who once settled this area. The Slovincians were skilled at adapting to the adversities of nature, as a visit to the museum reveals. One of their inventions consisted of eccentric-looking basket shoes to prevent their horses from sinking into the marshes.

★**Łeba** (pop. 4,000; 443km/277 miles) is better known as a resort than as a fishing and harbour town. The old fishermen's cottages have a lot of character, although almost every second house is a souvenir shop or a fish and chip shop. Łeba received a town charter as long ago as 1357, but it is more of a village outside the tourist season. The Łeba of those days was in fact 2km (1¼ miles) east of where it is now; shifting dunes and floods threatened to engulf the settlement, so in 1570 the inhabitants moved on to firmer ground.

Star Attractions
● **Dukes' Castles**
● **Kluki open-air museum**

Below: Kluki museum
Bottom: Słupsk Duke's Castle

Map on pages 32–3

Wdydzy Kiszewskie
One of Poland's earliest *skansens* (open-air museums), Wdydze Kiszewskie was established in 1906 within part of what is now the Wdydze Landscape Park. Reflecting the traditional arts and crafts of the Kashubian culture, furniture, wickerwork and embroidery continue to be produced in workshops here. The range of buildings in this extensive park include a manor house, wooden church, cottages, windmill and school.

NATURAL BEAUTY

For nature lovers and hikers the high point of this trip is the nearby ★★ **Słowinski National Park** (Słowinski Park Narodowy). The main attraction of this biosphere reserve, which covers an area of 18,000 hectares (44,500 acres), is its shifting dunes. They can be reached by rented bicycle or electric car, but if you want to climb up the huge hills of sand you must do so on foot. At a height of around 50m (164ft), the dunes are steadily moving, swallowing up even the forests in their path and, as a result, constitute one of the few desert areas in Europe. The park also includes two large lakes, Lake Łebsko and Lake Gardno. The latter is accessible to the public, but Lake Łebsko is a bird sanctuary, habitat of the rare great snipe.

THE BALTIC PENINSULA

Sandy beaches continue to feature along this route, and the next port of call is the famous ★★ **Hel Peninsula** (Mierzeja Helska). Around 200 years ago the present peninsula consisted of many small individual islands. In the course of time the sand washed in by the tides has linked them to create the current peninsula, which is only 200m (650ft) to 3km (1¾ miles) wide, but has a length of 35km (22 miles). It projects like a tongue out into the Gulf of Gdańsk and is a major tourist attraction.

The peninsula is still freely accessible by road, rail or ferry. However, this unique natural phenomenon is at risk from the curiosity of visitors and the action of the tides, so access may be limited in the near future. Dunes and pines are the dominant feature of the landscape, and the side facing the open sea, with its sandy beach, is ideal for bathing.

The 'capital' of the peninsula is ★ **Hel** (pop. 5,000; 558km/349 miles), situated at the far end of it. The road to the village passes through various historic fishing villages. Right on the harbour at Hel is a **Fishing Museum** (Muzeum Rybołówstwa) accommodated in a converted 15th-century church. With old fishermen's houses

Gardno Lake

dating from the 18th century, the smell of tar and seaweed and the hustle and bustle of the harbour, this little fishing village is full of atmosphere. Hel is also part of the homeland of the Kashubians, a Slavic people closely linked with Poland.

At this point, you may well feel tempted to go on a boat trip, if only on one of the ferries plying regularly between Hel, Gdańsk and Sopot. Car drivers, however, will prefer to complete the last stage of this route by land.

THE TRI-CITY

The outline of the industrial town and port of **Gdynia** soon appears in the distance; together with **Sopot** *(see page 50)* and **Gdańsk** (652km/ 408 miles, *next page*) it forms the so-called 'Tri-city', with a total population of around 800,000. These cities have grown to such an extent that they are virtually linked, though each has a totally individual character.

Gdańsk is the most historic and has the greatest range of architectural styles. Sopot has remained a traditional late 19th- and early 20th-century spa and seaside resort, while the port of Gdynia evolved from a fishing village in the 1930s. There are also various historic and cultural attractions within easy reach of the Tri-city, making it a good base for exploring the region.

Star Attractions
● **Słowinski National Park**
● **Hel Peninsula**

Below: Hel beach
Bottom: Sopot pier

Map on page 44

3: Gdańsk

Strolling through the streets of ornate and impressive historic buildings in Gdańsk (pop. 500,000), you can imagine yourself back in the medieval Hanseatic era, when a commercial alliance was formed between north German and Baltic cities for trade between the eastern and western sides of northern Europe *(see also box on page 34)*. Historically the key port on Poland's coastline, Gdańsk looks much as it did when it was built by wealthy merchants and ship owners. This impressive city was, however, a crowning achievement of Polish restoration. During World War II the city was more or less razed to the ground, and it took until 1975 to clear all the rubble and complete the reconstruction. But outward signs of prosperity conceal another story; in 1997 the Gdańsk shipyards were declared bankrupt.

Below: Old Town view from the Town Hall tower
Bottom: outdoor cafés on Long Market

HISTORY

'Gydanyzc' was mentioned in a document in 997 as a fortified settlement and the seat of a Slavic prince at the place where the River Motława flows into the Vistula, just before it enters the Baltic. It received a town charter in 1326, after it had already become a European trade centre that belonged to the Hanseatic League. The fact that

it had also been an object of dispute between various leaders is further evidence of Gdańsk's early importance. In 1308 the Teutonic Knights took over the town and founded a new settlement on its southern boundary that later became known as Główne Miasto, the Main Town.

After the decline of the Teutonic Knights, the independent towns united and in 1454 recognised Polish sovereignty. In its new form Gdańsk was able to negotiate an autonomous status with many privileges. The symbiosis with Poland also brought it great prosperity, as is evident from the splendid buildings which graced the town, then the largest in Poland, in the 16th and 17th centuries.

The restored restaurant Pod Łososiem (under the Salmon Restaurant) is a reminder of Gdańsk's position as a trading metropolis and meeting place for merchants from all over Europe. It was for them, in 1704, that an enterprising Dutchman opened the restaurant that was to become famous from Hamburg to Novgorod, compounding its fame with the invention of 'Gdańsk Goldwasser' (literally, gold water), a digestif vodka containing flakes of gold leaf that is still produced.

Gdańsk remained independent within the Polish-Lithuanian monarchy until the second partition of Poland in 1793, when it became Prussian.

From 1920 to 1939 Gdańsk, together with the surrounding areas of the Vistula island, became a free city and the residence of the high commissioner of the League of Nations. World War II, which began in Gdańsk, ended with disastrous consequences for the city: when in March 1945 joint units of the Red Army and the Polish army marched in, 90 percent of the historic buildings had been destroyed. The events in Gdańsk during World War II are vividly recreated by Günter Grass in his 1958 novel *The Tin Drum*.

SOLIDARITY

Forty years later Gdańsk once again came into the international spotlight, when Solidarity, a trade union movement against the Communist government, was formed. Gdańsk shipbuilders, led by

Goldwasser
The original reason for adding 23 carat gold leaf to Goldwasser vodka was the belief that it contained medicinal properties. Whether it contributed to the flavour is a matter of opinion, but with this vodka flavoured further with other ingredients this rich, digestif-style vodka offers plenty to savour on the palate. Goldwasser was also renowned as the most expensive vodka, giving it added cachet.

The Royal Chapel and Cathedral

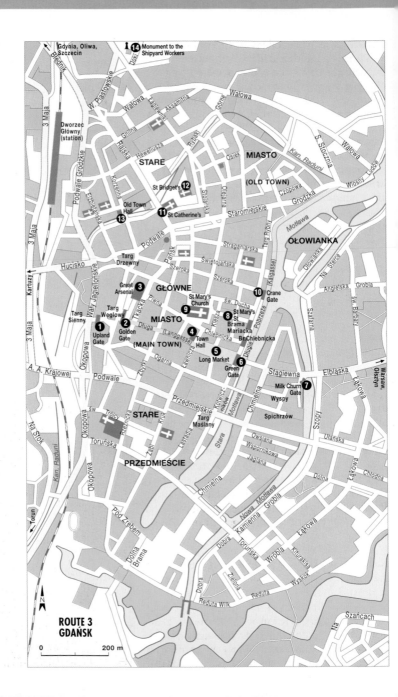

ROUTE 3
GDAŃSK

0   200 m

Lech Wałęsa, triggered public strikes to improve working conditions and in protest at massive price increases. In the 15 months of its activity from 1980, Solidarity proved to be a peaceful and powerful movement which, with 10 million members, represented the whole nation. However, on 13 December 1981, martial law was declared. Solidarity went underground and many of its leaders were imprisoned, starting a wave of repression.

The economic crisis worsened and the government proved unable to cope. However, under the leadership of Mikhail Gorbachev, the Soviet Union saw the beginnings of Perestroika and by the autumn of 1988, the party agreed to share political power. In June 1989, the first freely elected non-Communist Polish government took power. The Gdańsk shipyards, cradle of political reform throughout the former Eastern bloc, fell victim to the new free market economy.

SIGHTS

Walking round the reconstructed ★★ **Main Town** (Główne Miasto) today, it is hard to believe that at the end of World War II it had been reduced to ruins and rubble. Enter the town on the west side through the magnificent ★ **Upland Gate ❶** (Brama Wyżynna) built in 1588. This marks the start of the ★ **Royal Route**, along which the rulers formerly paraded into the town. By the gate is the recently opened Museum of Amber (Muzeum Bursztynu) open Mon–Sun 10am–8pm (6pm out of season). On the other side of the ★ **Golden Gate ❷** (Złota Brama), a Renaissance construction resembling a triumphal arch, is ★ **ulica Długa** or Long Street. Before continuing in the direction of the River Motława, make a detour to look at the ★ **Great Arsenal ❸** (Wielka Zbrojownia). This building, in the Mannerist style, now houses a supermarket. It is the work of the Dutchman Anthonis van Opbergen, an important Gdańsk architect, who also built the 'Hamlet Castle' Kronborg in Helsingor, Denmark. Back on Long Street, the fine residences on either side testify to the wealth of the merchants who built them. This includes the **Uphagen House**

Map opposite

Star Attraction
● Main Town, Gdańsk

Golden Gate

Map
on page
44

(Dom Uphagenow), at number 12, an 18th-century merchant's house which is a museum.

The ★ **Town Hall ④** (Ratusz) is a Gothic red brick building dating from the 14th century. The interior, which was restored at considerable cost and now houses the **Historical Museum of Gdańsk** (open Mon 10am–3pm, Tues–Sat 10am–6pm, Sun 11am–4pm), is worth a visit. The so-called Red Room is the most magnificent of the rooms: the large pictures covering walls and ceiling transform the whole interior into a single work of art. Most of this is original, since the furnishings were stored outside Gdańsk during the war.

Below: Artus Court,
Long Market
Bottom: town houses in
Piwna Street

LONG MARKET

Long Street opens out into ★★ **Long Market ⑤** (Długi Targ), a wide pedestrianised street lined with attractive burghers' houses, their showpiece facades dating from various epochs. One building stands out, with windows extending the full height of the lower part, which corresponds to three floors of the neighbouring houses. This is **Artus Court** (Dwór Artusa; open Mon 10am–3pm, Tues–Sat 10am–6pm, Sun 11am–6pm), which housed a stock exchange and the Merchant's Guild. In front of Artus Court, the 17th-century **Neptune Fountain** symbolises the importance of Gdańsk as a maritime power. The neighbouring **Golden House** (Złota

Kamiennica) is appropriately named, with a facade decorated in gilded reliefs. The **Green Gate ❻** (Zielona Brama) on the east side of Long Market marks the end of the Royal Route at the Motława, opposite an island featuring historic granaries and the **Milk Churn Gate ❼** (Baszty Mleczne). Its name comes from the shape of its round towers.

Star Attractions
● **Long Market**
● **St Mary's Street**

EXCURSIONS

If you have a boat trip in mind, the Green Gate is also the location of the **excursion boat quay** (przystań Zielona Brama). The boat ride takes you past the wharfs and the old fortress at the mouth of the Vistula and moors by the huge monument on Westerplatte – a reminder of the outbreak of World War II, when 182 soldiers held out for seven days against the Wehrmacht, defending a Polish ammunition depot on the peninsula.

Amber
Gdańsk has a huge number of boutiques, as well as street stalls selling various types of amber jewellery, including necklaces, rings, earrings and cuff links, not to mention objets d'art such as amber jewellery boxes and lamps. It is Poland's national stone, and many of the beaches in the Gdańsk area yield amber, which is washed up by the sea from below the sand.

ALONG THE WATERFRONT

Return to the waterfront (Długie Pobrzeże), and walk north past the 15th-century Bread Gate (Brama Chlebnicka) and St Mary's Gate (Brama Mariacka), which now houses the **Archaeological Museum** (Muzeum Archeologiczne; open Tue–Fri 9am–4pm, Sat–Sun 10am–4pm). The harbour quay was always more than just the place where cargo was loaded and unloaded, and it continues to play a commercial role, with boutiques selling amber jewellery and souvenirs alongside street traders and cafés.

On the other side of St Mary's Gate is the enchanting ★★ **St Mary's Street ❽** (ulica Mariacka) leading to St Mary's Church. The houses feature distinctive perrons, small terraces with steps leading down into the street, which were once a typical feature of towns on the Baltic coast. For the citizens of Gdańsk, they were a place to see and be seen. Today they have been taken over by amber boutiques and art galleries, and were also used in the filming of *Buddenbrooks* by Thomas Mann, since no such street could be found in Lubeck, where the book is actually set.

Baltic amber for sale

Map on page 44

Below: by the Motława River Bottom: St Mary's astrological clock

HISTORIC ST MARY'S

★★ **St Mary's Church ⑨** (Kościół Mariacki) is one of the largest churches in Europe, with a vaulted ceiling 30m (98ft) high. This Gothic church was built between 1343 and 1502, and can accommodate almost 25,000 worshippers. The beautiful vaulting is a key feature, along with numerous Gothic altars, Renaissance and baroque elements, and an extraordinary medieval astrological clock. The so-called 'Beautiful Madonna' is the most impressive sculpture.

The work given most attention by the guides is the triptych *The Last Judgement* (1466–73) by Hans Memling. The picture was commandeered by citizens of Gdańsk en route to the person for whom it was painted in Tuscany; they put it up in St Mary's as war booty. What the visitor sees now, however, is a copy: the original is to be found in the **Gdańsk National Museum** (Muzeum Narodowe; open Tues–Fri 9am–4pm, Sat–Sun 10am–4pm) in the former Franciscan monastery near the Church of the Holy Trinity.

Returning to the harbour promenade you cannot miss the 15th-century ★★ **Crane Gate ⑩** (Żuraw). The enormous harbour crane is one of the largest medieval industrial constructions in existence and now houses the **Central Maritime Museum** (Centralne Muzeum Morskie). The Crane Gate is the symbol of Gdańsk. It is typical of this

trading city that it was not one of the churches but a secular building that was chosen for this honour.

OLD TOWN

A few minutes further to the north is the former **Old Town** which also features numerous historic buildings reconstructed after World War II. Jan Heweliusz, or Johannes Hevelius (1611–1686), who published one of the first detailed maps of the moon, is buried in the Gothic and baroque parish church, **St Catherine's** ⓫ (Kościół Św Katarzyny). Since he earned little money from his astronomy, Heweliusz also worked as a brewer; today 'Hevelius' beer is as popular as ever.

The church immediately behind it, ★ **St Bridget's** ⓬ (Kościół Św Brygidy), went down in recent Polish history as the 'Solidarity Church', since it was here that the anti-Communist opposition met to worship when the country was under martial law, as an expression of political disobedience. The tasteful modern interior combines surprisingly well with the reconstructed Gothic star vaulting.

The tour of Gdańsk ends at the **Old Town Hall** ⓭ (Ratusz Starego Miasta) completed in 1595, where various historic artefacts can be seen.

SHIPYARDS

A small detour in the direction of the shipyards will bring you to the ★★ **Monument to the Shipyard Workers** ⓮ (Pomnik Stoczniowców Poległych). The three huge crosses set up near Gate 2 of the Gdańsk shipyards commemorate the 28 people who died when the strike in December 1970 was brutally suppressed.

The monument was erected in 1980 by Solidarity, and even when the organisation was subsequently outlawed, the Communist leaders did not dare touch the memorial because of its powerful symbolic significance. Drogi do Wolności (Roads to Freedom) is a museum within easy reach of the shipyard tracing the history of the Solidarity movement (www.wystawa.fcs.org.pl).

Star Attractions
● St Mary's Church
● Crane Gate
● Monument to the Shipyard Workers

Rising from the ruins
Gdańsk suffered not only during the Nazi invasion and occupation, but also the further devastation that followed when the city was liberated by the Red Army. Many historic buildings were completely obliterated and had to be reconstructed from ruins. The skill with which this was done is immediately evident. The result is a beautiful city.

Monument to the Shipyard Workers

Map on page 44

Map on page 44

Joseph Conrad
A poignant statue of the novelist Joseph Conrad (1857–1926) stands in Gdynia, looking out to sea. This is particularly appropriate for a Polish-born novelist who wrote many books with a maritime theme, including *Lord Jim*, *Nostromo* and *Heart of Darkness*. Learning English later in life, and spending the second half of his life in England, he ranks as one of the finest modern novelists writing in the English language.

Dar Pomorza
training ship

SUBURBS

From the main station, take a taxi, bus or tram to the suburbs of Oliwa, Sopot and Gdynia. **Oliwa** was founded by the Cistercian order in 1188. Its ★★ **Cathedral** (Katedra Oliwska), rebuilt a number of times, dates from the 13th century and was originally the monastery church. The interior, 100m (330ft) long, has 16th and 17th century artefacts. Its wonderful acoustics are demonstrated when the splendid 18th-century baroque ★ **organ** is played; short recitals are given regularly during the day. It has 7,876 pipes and mechanised figures which move when the organ is played. An international organ festival is held in Oliwa every August.

SOPOT

★ **Sopot**, close to Oliwa, has been one of the most fashionable seaside resorts and spas since the 19th century and is still a popular spot for tourists. The Secessionist villas reflect the former lifestyle of the upper classes, set along broad avenues with frequent greenery creating a relaxed atmosphere. The pier extends 500m (1,640ft) out into the Baltic and is the longest in Poland. The Grand Hotel, set by the beach, is an example of Art Nouveau elegance, along with the original casino. Bohaterów Monte Casino is a key promenade, with shops and cafés, in the centre of Sopot.

GDYNIA

Gdynia, the next town, contrasts with the villas of Sopot. The city – now the industrial quarter of the Tri-city – developed between the wars as a Polish port in competition with the Free City of Gdańsk, which was not then part of Poland. Moored at the pier is the World War II destroyer *Błyskawica*, which is now a museum ship, and the famous sailing-school ship *Dar Pomorza*, a three-masted frigate dating from 1909. A statue of Joseph Conrad, born Jozef Korzeniowski, looks out longingly to sea: with this monument, Gdynia pays tribute to the great British author of Polish origin, who wrote *Lord Jim* and other maritime novels.

4: East to the Masurian Lakes

Gdańsk – Malbork – Elbląg – Olsztyn – Mrągowo – Gizycko – Mikołajki – Lake Luknajno (416km/260 miles)

Map on page 52

Crystal-clear lakes, unspoilt forests, enchanting landscapes and the occasional village – this is what holidaymakers who want to get away from it all can find. Masuria, Poland's 'green lung', has all the natural beauty to make it the most popular holiday region in Poland. For anglers, hikers and watersports enthusiasts, this 'land of a thousand lakes' is the perfect destination.

Allow around seven days for this route, which leads through Malbork and Elbląg to Olsztyn in the historic region of Warmia, and further into the heart of the Masurian Lake District in the Mikołajki region. The most convenient form of transport for this route is obviously a car, but if you have the energy – and, naturally, the time – the best way to see the region is by bicycle: Masuria is a cyclists' paradise.

Many places in Masuria have good tourist facilities. However, if you do not book in advance, it may be difficult to find vacancies in Western-standard hotels in the peak holiday season. The most appropriate form of accommodation on this trip is a tent, which is not only cheap but the best way to experience the natural beauty of the countryside.

*Below and bottom:
Malbork Castle*

Malbork

From Gdańsk take the E75 south for 58km (36 miles) to **Malbork** (pop. 40,000). The town is known as the site of one of the most famous buildings in Europe, ★★★**Malbork Castle** (open Tues–Sun 9am–7pm 1 May–30 Sept, then Tues–Sun 10am–3pm), also one of Europe's largest fortified sites. The infamous and powerful Teutonic Knights had their headquarters in the red brick castle (known in German as Marienburg), which is idyllically set on the steep banks of the River Nogat. It creates a truly impressive sight.

Dating from the 13th and 14th centuries, it is entered through the Lower Castle, which incor-

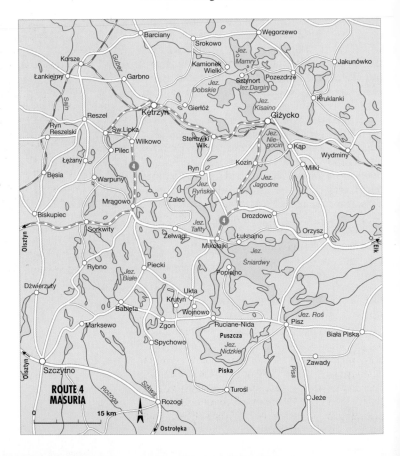

porates the arsenal and St Lawrence Chapel. In the adjoining Middle Castle is the **palace of the Grand Master** – later used occasionally as a residence by the Polish king and his governors – the Great Refectory and the rooms formerly used for the knights' guests.

A bridge leads across to the High Castle where the knights themselves lived. Together with the chapter hall, the castle's church will be one of the most outstanding features when restoration work has been completed. For the moment visitors have to content themselves with the **Golden Gate**, the doorway of the church, which is richly decorated with mythical beasts.

A tower, which is connected to the castle by a passage can be seen off to the side of the complex near the river. This is the Gdańisko Tower, which, for those less well versed in medieval castle architecture, was simply a large latrine, hence its position not within the walls but at a discreet 'safe distance' outside. Here the Nogat functioned as the natural sewerage system.

The only way to see around the castle is by joining one of the lengthy guided tours. In the west wing of the **Middle Castle** is a permanent exhibition on the origins and craftsmanship of amber. Many visitors will be surprised to discover that this 'Baltic gold' is actually fossilised resin from conifer trees dating back to the Eocene epoch. Made into valuable jewellery, it brought great prosperity to the coastal towns. Today amber jewellery and various objets d'art are the most popular souvenirs from Poland.

Star Attractions
● **Malbork Castle**

Teutonic Knights
The Teutonic Knights were a military order of German knights who served in the Holy Land. They played an important part in Polish history, originally acquiring their prosperity through gifts of land for their hospital work during the Crusades. They were also given land in northeast Poland in 1225 in return for assisting the Mazovian Duke Konrad to repel an invasion of pagan Prussians. After annexing this Prussian territory, they gradually extended their occupation, invading Polish towns such as Gdańsk in the early 14th century and slaughtering the inhabitants, until their incursions were finally repulsed by the joint Polish-Lithuanian Commonwealth, and they were defeated in 1410 at the famous Battle of Grunwald. Malbork Castle, established as the headquarters of the knights' grand master, was taken over by the Poles in 1457 and the Grand Master swore allegiance to the Polish king.

ELBLĄG

Elbląg (pop. 120,000; 100km/60 miles from Malbork) is situated on the Baltic coast. Because of its ideal location, the town has changed hands several times over the centuries, and was often destroyed by the victors in the process. Pagan Prussians and German knights, Prussians and Poles, Swedes and Russians all coveted the Baltic port, and at the end of World War II Elbląg had been reduced to rubble.

Map on page 52

The Old Town includes some buildings which have been reconstructed in their original form, on the basis of historic documents, while the restoration of the rest remains an ongoing project. **The City Museum** (Muzeum W Elblągu; open Tues–Sun 9am–5pm) details the history of Elbląg.

For 40 years the harbour could not be used: the only exit to the Baltic from the Vistula Lagoon (Zalew Wiślany) was at the Russian town of Baltijsk, access to which was prohibited by the Baltic fleet that was stationed there. As a result, Elbląg could not be reached by water. The hydrofoils that now ply between Elbląg and Kaliningrad have become a popular tourist attraction.

The town of Elbląg is best known for its canal, the ★★ **Kanał Ostrodzko-Elbląski** (trips along this 80-km/50-mile waterway to Ostroda start during the season from Elbląg at 8am). Built in 1858, it is the only canal in the world where the boats travel overland as well as on the water. This marvel of technology navigates height differences of almost 100m (330ft) and includes so-called 'inclined planes', which are used to haul boats overland.

Below: Elbląski canal
Bottom: a boat on rails

FROMBORK

The small town of **Frombork**, 32km (20 miles) north of Elbląg on the Vistula Lagoon, is well

worth a detour. It has a 14th-century Gothic ★★ **cathedral** (open Mon–Sat 9.30am–5pm) perched on a hill with a courtyard, surrounded by fortified walls and towers. Its distinctive and ornate facade, flanked by two slim towers, is best viewed from one of the fortified towers. The palace (open Tues–Sun 9am–4.30pm), and the Planetarium (open Mon–Sat 9.30am–5pm) are among the other attractions.

A CHANGE OF SCENE

Continue to **Pasłęk** (pop. 10,000; 122km/76 miles). Dutch colonists developed this area in the 14th century by building dams and applying successful drainage techniques. Fill your picnic basket at Pasłęk's well-stocked delicatessens, ready for a picnic by the canal (follow the sign marked 'Sluza Buczyniec 8km' on the outskirts of the town, behind the new petrol station). Have your cameras ready at 12.20pm to capture a picture of a vessel being hauled overland.

Drive through the village of Drulity to Morzewo and return to the E77 which will bring you in no time to **Ostroda** (pop. 35,000), the starting point for canoe tours.

HISTORIC BATTLEFIELD

The next stop is **Grunwald** (200km/125 miles), Poland's most famous battlefield. On 15 July 1410, the combined Polish-Lithuanian army inflicted a crushing defeat on the Teutonic Knights in the Battle of Grunwald, one of the biggest and fiercest of battles in the Middle Ages. A monument erected in 1960 commemorates this key event in Polish history, which liberated the country from the influence of the knights.

The history trail continues in nearby **Olsztynek** (pop. 15,000; 226km/141 miles), whose main attraction is the ★ **open-air museum** *(skansen)*. Set in beautiful countryside are examples of historic peasants' houses from Masuria and Warmia. The museum is at the northeastern exit of the town so there is no need to leave the route to Olsztyn.

Star Attractions
● Ostrodzko-Elblaski Canal
● Frombork Cathedral

Teutonic castles
The Teutonic Knights constructed a network of castles as their influence grew in Poland. The locations were carefully chosen to ensure that no more than one day's journey on horseback was required to reach one castle from another, which also means that following a 'Teutonic trail' is easy with modern transport.

Frombork cathedral

Map
on page
52

Hiking country
An ideal way to enjoy the beautiful natural scenery of the Masurian region is by hiking. Rather than creating your own itinerary, there are numerous marked trails that you can follow. Some of these have specific themes, such as the Copernicus Trail from Olsztyn to Frombork, a total of 170km (106 miles), while a shorter trail of 10km (6 miles) takes you from Iława to Szyrnbark.

Lidzbark Warmiński Castle

A MASURIAN CAPITAL

Olsztyn (pop. 150,000; 251km/156 miles) has a reconstructed ★ **Old Town**, providing artists and craftsmen with an attractive setting for their studios and galleries.

After a walk around the Old Town, time should be left for a visit to the 14th-century ★ **Castle** *(zamek)*, which now houses the **Warmia and Masuria Regional Museum** (Muzeum Warmii i Mazur; open Tues–Sun 9am–5pm June–Aug, otherwise 10am–4pm) with its art and natural science collections. The unusual stone figures standing in the castle courtyard are idols once worshipped by the pagan Prussians and date from the early Middle Ages. They are all that has remained of the people to whom this country once belonged.

The ★ **Cathedral of St James** (Kościół Św Jakuba) was built at the same time as the castle. The most outstanding feature is the Gothic star and net vaulting which elegantly patterns the ceiling. Olsztyn's modern attraction is the **Copernicus Planetarium** in the aleja Zwycięstwa, where outer space is shown not from the perspective of the Earth's inhabitants but from that of the astronauts (open Tues–Fri 10am–4pm June–Aug, otherwise Mon–Fri 12–4pm, Sat–Sun 10.30am–4pm).

A BISHOP'S CASTLE

★ **Lidzbark Warmiński Castle**, just under 50km (31 miles) north of Olsztyn, was built after 1350, as the residence of the Warmian bishops. Next to Malbork Castle it is the most impressive building in the region. The excellently preserved rooms feature fine vaulting and original wall paintings.

SORKWITY

From Olsztyn the route follows national highway 16 in an easterly direction. Make the most of this attractive stretch of road and take time to stop off in one of the many picturesque spots en route. After 50km (31 miles) you will arrive at **Sorkwity** (pop. 900; 301km/188 miles). Shortly after entering the village you will see the whitewashed ★ **village**

church on the left-hand side of the road. This is one of the few Protestant churches in Masuria today. The pastor, who lives opposite the church, will gladly open the building and point out its proudest possession, a colourful baptismal angel hovering high above the heads of the faithful near the ceiling of the nave. With the help of a block-and-tackle construction, the wooden sculpture can be lowered at christenings so that the head of the child being christened can be moistened with holy water from the silver dish it holds.

★★**Sorkwity Palace**, a picture-book palace in 19th-century 'neo-Renaissance' style, is set in suitably enchanting surroundings in the midst of historic oak trees on the shore of Lake Lampackie.

Further along the route lies **Mrągowo** (pop. 21,000; 313km/196 miles), nestling in beautiful countryside. And from here the classic tourist destinations, such as the Roman Catholic shrine, Święta Lipka, and the largest of the Masurian Lakes can be reached in a day.

Below: a lake near Mrągowo
Bottom: Święta Lipka

ŚWIĘTA LIPKA

A must on every tour of Masuria is a visit to the shrine of **Święta Lipka** (literally the Holy Lime Tree). The 15-km (9-mile) trip over moraines and along the shores of beautiful lakes is in itself worthwhile. Hikers staying in Mrągowo will want

Map on page 52

to take the 22-km (14-mile) trail that leads to the shrine, where the 17th-century ★★**pilgrims' church**, a splendid ochre-coloured baroque building with two towers and a facade ornamented with columns and sculptures, stands in a secluded area. Every hour the **18th-century organ** is played, setting in motion the small biblical figures which are attached to the instrument.

KĘTRZYN

Below: Lake Łuknajno
Bottom: Hitler's bunker

It is only 14km (9 miles) from here to **Kętrzyn** (349km/218 miles), where, a few kilometres to the east, near the village of Gierłoz in the middle of the forest, is a huge bunker complex constructed from steel and concrete that was once the headquarters of Adolf Hitler. Hitler occupied this compound, known as the 'Wolf's Lair', for almost two years, directing much of his war strategy from here. It was here, on 20 July 1944, that Klaus Graf Schenk von Stauffenberg exploded a bomb in a courageous, though unsuccessful, attempt to assassinate Hitler, who was out of the room at the time. At the kiosk is a plan of the complex and guides are available.

GIŻYCKO

The ★★**Masurian landscape** is made up of thousands of lakes and majestic hills. In the rushes along

the banks of the lakes, swans, cranes, herons, crested divers and ducks find safe nesting places. The waters are teeming with eels, pike and salmon trout.

Giżycko (pop. 28,000; 381km/238 miles) is one of the most popular holiday centres in Masuria, in an idyllic location between two lakes: Niegocin in the south and Kisajno in the north (actually part of Lake Mamry). In 1772 a canal was built between the two lakes, a route which today is used almost exclusively by water-sports enthusiasts. Excursion boats provide an ideal way to enjoy the scenery, linking the town with Mikołajki (4½ hours) and Węgorzewo (2½ hours).

MIKOŁAJKI

★★**Mikołajki** (pop. 4,000; 416km/260 miles) is fondly referred to as the 'Masurian Venice'. It is a particularly beautiful town, and in the holiday season tourists are in the majority, as they have been for the last 100 years. Close to the largest Masurian lake, Lake Śniardwy, it is an Eldorado for nature lovers and water-sports fans. Excursion boats leave from Mikołajki for trips on the larger lakes.

An interesting point at which to end this tour may be **Lake Łuknajno**, 5km (3 miles) east of Mikołajki. Every summer the lake is home to thousands of wild swans and herons, which can be seen from an observation centre.

KRUTYN

Krutyn, a small place near Ukta south of Mikołajki, is situated on what is probably the most picturesque river in Masuria, the Krutynia, and is well-known among canoeists. The ★ **punting trips** organised from Krutyn are greatly recommended. Leave the punting to the local boatman and enjoy this splendid, tranquil waterway. The green tunnel and shimmering red stones, over which the crystal-clear water of the river flows, will be a treasured memory.

To the southeast lies the **Puszcza Piska**, a wilderness of primeval fir and pine forest supporting a variety of wildlife, including wild boar and bison.

Star Attractions
● Pilgrims' Church
● Masurian landscape
● Mikołajki

Further east
Travelling further east from the Masurian lake district leads to the Wigierski National Park. Two ideal bases for exploring the park are Suwałki and Angustów, with various routes through the park. With more than 40 lakes, six rivers, pine and spruce forests and peat bogs, the park is a habitat for rare species, including European beavers.

On the river near Krutyn

Map on pages 66–7

5: Along the Vistula

Gdańsk – Chełmno – Toruń – Płock – Warsaw (406km/254 miles)

This route follows Poland's principal river, the Vistula. It leads from Gdańsk (*see pages 42–9*) to Warsaw, passing through places of great historic significance such as Toruń. It is a journey through the 1,000-year history and culture of the country, with the capital of Poland undoubtedly a high point of the trip, contrasting history and modernism, and is designed to take three days.

PELPLIN

Poland's principal river

The River Vistula (Wisła) extends for virtually the entire length of central Poland, originating in the south and continuing all the way to the Baltic Sea. En route, the river passes through various towns and cities which are popular tourist destinations. These include Cracow, Sandomierz, Warsaw, Płock and Toruń.

Spring blossom near Sandomierz

Outside ★ **Gniew**, which has a medieval Teutonic Knights' castle and town hall, is the old Cistercian abbey of **Pelplin**, only 4km (2½ miles) from the main road. The ★ **Cathedral of the Blessed Virgin Mary**, dating from the 14th century, has a fine ceiling with elaborate vaulting among 15th- to 18th-century interiors.

Under an hour's drive further on, there is a fine panoramic view of **Grudziądz** (pop. 100,000; 113km/71 miles) on the other side of the Vistula. The Prussian citadel, completed in 1788, is set amidst towers and defensive walls. The buildings fronting the river are a complex of 26 granaries dating from the 14th to 18th centuries.

Gothic and baroque churches and the Benedictine Abbey are also impressive features.

CHEŁMNO

One of the most attractive sections of this route continues through lush meadows on the east bank of the Vistula. Take time over this section and take a walk down to the river, close to the medieval town of **Chełmno** (pop. 22,000; 145km/91 miles), the next stop. A must for anyone interested in Polish history, Chełmno had its heyday as a centre for trading grain and producing wool between the 13th and 15th centuries when it belonged to the Hanseatic League *(see page 42)*.

Before exploring the ★★ **Old Town** perched on the high banks of the Vistula and visible from a distance, learn about the city's past in the **Regional Museum**. This is located in the market square in the **Town Hall** (Ratusz), a 16th-century building in the Italian Renaissance style, one of the finest and northernmost examples of this type of architecture, which spread here from Cracow. Its unusual structure features a large, ornamental attic and windows which diminish in size towards the bottom of the building, literally turning the ancient theory of proportions on its head. Also in the market square, with its distinctive outline, is the **Church of the Assumption of the Blessed Virgin Mary** (Kościół Wniebowzięcia NMP). It was built from 1280–1320 and features Gothic frescoes in the choir and the 14th-century figures of 11 apostles. The Old Town is encircled by the city wall, which dates from the 14th century. Other Gothic churches, several bastions and the Grudiądz Gate (Brama Grudiądzka) have all remained, showing the original medieval layout of the town.

TORUŃ

This route leaves the Vistula for a short time and takes the direct route on the E75. The river, curving west, skirts the large industrial town of Bydgoszcz, which has an Old Town with historic granaries on the waterfront.

Star Attraction
● Chełmno Old Town

Below: Chełmno Town Hall
Bottom: on the banks
of the Vistula

Map on pages 66–7

Below: statue of Copernicus, Toruń
Bottom: Toruń Old Town

★★ **Toruń** (pop. 205,000; 190km/119 miles), has an ensemble of Gothic architecture that is unique in Europe. In 1233 the Teutonic Knights founded a castle on the banks of the Vistula as a centre for military operations against the Prussians. Toruń joined the Hanseatic League at the end of the 13th century *(see page 34)* and had trading partners as far away as Holland. Growing pressure from the merchants of Toruń for greater independence brought them into conflict with the authoritarian Teutonic Knights. In 1455 the conflict came to a head with the citizens of Toruń storming the castle and partially destroying it (the ruins can be visited; open 9am–dusk daily). The city then acknowledged the sovereignty of the Polish king but was astute enough to negotiate its own autonomy.

OLD TOWN

The varied buildings of the ★★ **Old Town** are within a compact area. The market square is dominated by the ★ **Town Hall** (Ratusz), which has survived intact. This red brick building originates from the 13th century and was subsequently enlarged to its present form with a central courtyard. It now houses the **Regional Museum** (Muzeum Okręgowe; open Tues–Sun 10am–6pm 1 May–30 Sept, otherwise Tues–Sun 10am–4pm).

In front of the Town Hall is the **statue of**

Copernicus. The renowned astronomer Nicolas Copernicus (Mikołaj Kopernik, 1473–1543) is Toruń's most famous son and is still celebrated as one of history's greatest scientists. The nearby **Copernicus Museum** (Dom Kopernika; open Tues–Sun 10am–6pm, 1 May–31 Aug, otherwise Tues–Sun 10am– 4pm), ulica Kopernika 15–17, furnishes the proof: the 15th-century Gothic house where Copernicus is said to have been born houses a comprehensive collection of exhibits relating to him, including the original edition of *De revolutionibus orbium Coelestium* (1543). With this book Copernicus refuted the Church's doctrine that the earth was the centre of the universe.

On the east side of the market square is a burgher's house dating from 1697, the House under the Star (Kamiennica pod Gwiazdą), which is now the **Museum of Far Eastern Art** (open Tues–Sun 10am–6pm, until 4pm during the winter). Nearby, in the direction of the Vistula stands the massive tower of ★ **St John's Church** (Kościół Św Jana). The church with its distinctive roofs dates from the 14th century; the famous *Beautiful Madonna* on the north wall of the apse is a copy of the original statue, which disappeared during World War II, but the early Gothic frescoes in the choir have been preserved in their original form.

The Old Town also has other impressive Gothic and baroque churches, including the neo-baroque Church of the Holy Spirit (Kościół Św Ducha, 1754–56) with its 64-m (210-ft) tower. **St Mary's Church** (Kościół Najświętszej Maryii Panny) is a Gothic building which, in accordance with the regulations of the Franciscan order, has no tower at all. Dating from 1351, the outstanding features are the beautiful frescoes on the south wall – the church seems very high because the naves are so narrow. The baroque altar and Mannerist sarcophagi of members of the Toruń nobility can also be seen in the southern nave.

CIECHOCINEK

Cross back over the Vistula and drive a further 22km (14 miles) on the E75 to ★★ **Ciechocinek**.

Star Attractions
● **Toruń's Old Town**
● **Ciechocinek**

Toruń's *skansen*
A delightful rural oasis in the city centre, the *skansen* is a recreation of a village, showing the regional architectural style through a range of 19th-century wooden buildings, complete with original furniture and interior decoration. This includes peasant's cottages and typical farmhouses with outbuildings and even kennels. A large barn provides an atmospheric setting for temporary exhibitions of folk art. Open 15 Apr–30 Sept: Mon, Wed, Fri 9am–4pm, Tues, Thur, Sat, Sun 10am–6pm; otherwise Tues–Fri, 9am–4pm, Sat–Sun 10am–4pm.

The Church of the Holy Spirit, Toruń

Map on pages 66-7

The spa tradition

Throughout Poland are scattered spa towns, such as Ciechocinek, which have provided various health benefits for centuries. Spas were also visited for the social benefits they offered, which explains why spa towns have other historic buildings worth visiting which served different purposes. At Ciechocinek, for example, there is a concert hall dating from 1903, constructed from wood in the Zakopane style, modelled on the traditional style of southern Poland's Highlanders *(see page 84)*.

The main attraction of this spa town is the graduation tower dating from 1830, said to be the oldest and largest in the world. This fulfils a therapeutic function: the air in its vicinity has a high salt and mineral content which has a beneficial effect on those suffering from respiratory diseases, and this is also said to increase general wellbeing.

The climate of **Włocławek** (pop. 110,000; 246km/154 miles) is anything but beneficial. The industrial metropolis with its paper and china factories, which discharge their waste water into the Vistula, is largely responsible for the catastrophic pollution in the river. Włocławek is nevertheless worth visiting for its **cathedral**. Begun in the 14th century, the church houses the marble sarcophagus of Bishop Piotr of Bnin, which was the work of the Nuremberg artist Veit Stoss in 1493.

PŁOCK

Shortly before Warsaw, make a final stop in ★ **Płock** (pop. 135,000; 296km/185 miles). Płock is not only a centre of the oil industry, it also attracts tourists with its clifftop castle above the Vistula. The ★ **castle and cathedral** complex dates from the 11th century, although the sumptuous interior of the Romanesque cathedral is more recent, dating from the 19th century; the Royal Chapel contains the sarcophagi of two Polish rulers Władysław I Herman and his son Bolesław III Krzywousty (the Wry-mouthed). Although they are copies, the Płock Bronze Doors are an interesting feature. The originals were made for Płock in the 12th century but, as a result of a mysterious conflict, found their way to Russia where, as the Novgorod Bronze Doors, they embellish the Cathedral of St Sophia.

In the castle, once the seat of the Mazovian dukes, the Mazovian Museum's **Art Nouveau Collection** (Muzeum Mazowieckie, Zbiory Secesji; open Tues–Sun 10am–5pm, in summer, Tues 10am–3pm, Wed–Fri 10am–4pm, Sat–Sun 11.30am–4.30 in winter), incorporating crafts, furniture and paintings, is one of the best of its kind. Warsaw *(see page 20)* is a further 110km (68 miles).

Płock cathedral

6: Cradle of the Polish State

Warsaw – Gniezno – Poznań – Łagów (522km/ 326 miles)

This route runs in more or less a straight line from east to west, taking in Gniezno, which goes back 1,000 years, and Poznań, a city second only to Warsaw in terms of commercial stature. It ends in the idyllic countryside on the eastern border with Germany. Three days should be allowed in all. Finding hotel rooms in Poznań may be difficult whenever the city is hosting one of its frequent trade fairs, so it is advisable to make reservations in advance. The journey begins in Warsaw.

This region was originally the seat of the Piast dukes, who became the first kings of Poland after uniting the leaders of various neighbouring duchies. Mieszko I, the first Piast king, converted the country to Christianity in AD 966 and Gniezno was established as the first bishopric in 1000. The city was the first capital of Poland, which it remained until 1038, when the capital was transferred to Cracow.

NIEBORÓW

After 77km (48 miles) take the left-hand turning to Nieborów. The baroque ★★ **palace** of Nieborów (open Mon–Sun 10am–4pm March–April; Mon–Sun 10am–8pm May–June, Mon–Fri 10am–4pm,

Map on pages 66–7

Star Attraction
● Nieborów Palace

Below: the Virgin outside Nieborów parish church
Bottom: Nieborów palace

Map below

Sat–Sun 10am–6pm; Tues–Sun 10am–3.30pm Oct), designed by Tylman van Gameren and surrounded by an extensive park, is one of Poland's finest examples of early 18th-century architecture. Until 1945 it belonged to the Radziwiłł's, a wealthy Polish-Lithuanian aristocratic family.

The palace has a comprehensive collection of objets d'art, though this is rather eccentrically arranged with antique sculptures next to fine hand-

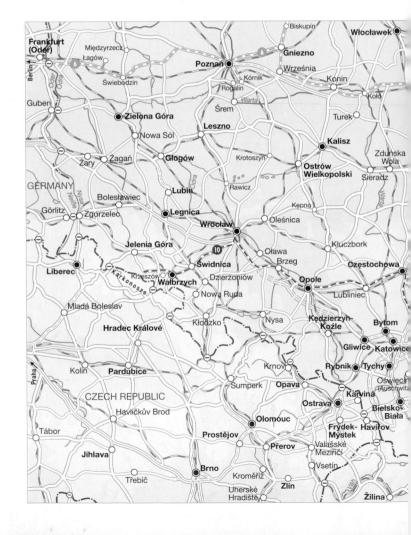

icraft exhibits. Among the sculptures set around the palace's beautiful park is the notable *Stone Women*, which was brought from the steppes on the shores of the Baltic Sea.

Star Attraction
● Arkadia

ARCADIAN EXPERIENCE

The name of the next village, ★★ **Arkadia**, is very evocative. The renowned park (open daily 10am–

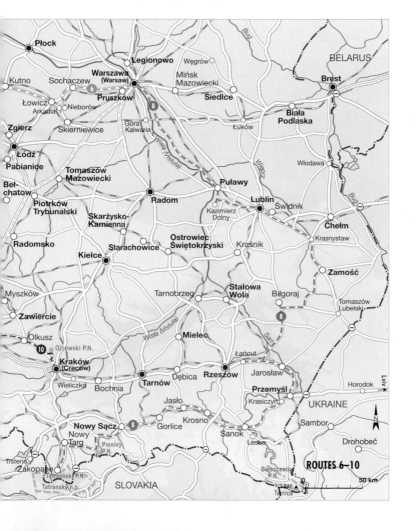

ROUTES 6–10

Map on pages 66–7

dusk) here owes its existence to Helena Radiz-wiłł, whose longing for the legendary Arcadia motivated her to create a paradise on this spot. The picturesque landscaped garden with lakes and a stream has its own special charm, and the picture is completed by a neoclassical Temple of Diana, an aqueduct and a ruined castle.

ŁOWICZ

The best time to visit ★ **Łowicz** (pop. 30,000; 91km/57 miles) is Corpus Christi, which usually falls around the beginning of June. The town is renowned for its colourful procession on this feast day, when the people of Łowicz proudly present themselves in their famous regional costumes.

A historic trading city dating from the 12th century, Łowicz is known for its traditional folk arts and crafts: the wood carvings, silhouettes and brightly coloured handwoven materials remain in demand all over the country. The ethnographic section of the ★ **Regional Museum** has a comprehensive collection of exhibits illustrating the customs and traditional crafts of the region, including folk art paper cut-outs. The museum is housed in the former Missionary College, a baroque building in the town centre.

The **Collegiate Church** dating from 1668 is worth a visit for its rich baroque decoration and the

Below: 'Welcome to Łowicz'
Bottom: Arkadia

Old Town still has numerous historic burghers' houses dating from the 18th and 19th centuries.

LĄD

In the village of **Ląd**, 30km (20 miles) west of Konin, is a particularly beautiful monastery set in picturesque countryside by the Warta. ★ **Ląd Monastery** should on no account be missed: founded in 1175 by Cistercian monks, it was repeatedly extended and reconstructed over the following six centuries. The present abbey church is a combination of Gothic and Baroque. The interior's early 14th-century wall paintings are among the finest examples in Poland.

GNIEZNO

The route now continues via side roads, first in a northerly direction to **Gniezno** (pop. 70,000; 285km/ 178 miles), which is an absolute must on your trip. Gniezno was the first capital of the Kingdom of Poland, and it was in AD1000 that the German Emperor Otto III and Bolesław I Chrobry (the Brave) met here. On that occasion, Otto not only sanctioned the establishment of the archbishopric of Gniezno but also promised to support the coronation of Bolesław as king of the new state of Poland.

Built on hills, the town is dominated by the 14th-century ★★ **Cathedral of the Assumption of the Blessed Virgin Mary and St Adalbert** (Katedra Wniebowzięcia NMP i Św Wojciecha; open Mon–Sat 9am–11am, 1pm–5pm, Sun 1pm–3pm), closed to tourists during Mass). It is the most monumental Gothic church in Poland and outstanding among its treasures are the Romanesque bronze doors (in the western part of the south nave), dating from 1170, which were probably cast in Liège workshops. On the doors are reliefs illustrating the life of St Adalbert, who ranks alongside St Stanislaus as the most important saint in Poland as well as in Bohemia. In 18 scenes, the Prague bishop Adalbert is depicted leaving Gniezno in 997 to baptise the pagan Prussians, celebrating Mass and preaching,

Star Attraction
● **Gniezno Cathedral**

Sacral artefacts
In addition to the splendour of Gniezno Cathedral's interiors, the cathedral's treasury has an extraordinary collection of sacral art and relics. This includes numerous chalices, with Gothic, Renaissance and baroque examples, together with candlesticks, crucifixes and relics from various saints, such as St Barbara and St Adalbert.

Gniezno cathedral

Map on pages 66–7

The Lednica *skansen*
Located between Gniezno and Poznań, Ostrów Lednicki is the setting of the first Piast Museum. The park includes a *skansen* (open-air) museum, with the late 10th-century remains of the earliest brick constructions in Poland, including a palace and chapel. To the south is the Piast stronghold (Gród Piastowski) in Giecz, which also has remains from the 10th century, including stone architecture and embankments.

and then finally being killed by them with axes and spears, after which the later King Bolesław Chrobry is shown buying his body for its equivalent weight in gold. St Adalbert is buried in a silver sarcophagus in the centre of the main nave.

Adjoining the cathedral is the **Museum of the Archdiocese of Gniezno** (Muzeum Archidiecezi Gnieźeńskiej; open Tues–Sun 9am–5.30pm), which has a comprehensive range of ecclesiastical items and sacral art. **The Museum of the Origins of the Polish State** (Muzeum Początków Państwa Polskiego, Kostrzewskiego 1; open Tues–Sun 10am–5pm) details the evolution and importance of the city.

BISKUPIN

The next stop, **Biskupin**, will take you even further back in history. The village, 38km (24 miles) north of Gniezno, is famous for its archaelogical finds from the 6th century BC. In the Iron Age a tribe of the vanished Lusatian culture built a ★ **fortified village** on an island in Lake Biskupin that has now become a peninsula. The settlement has been partially reconstructed.

To get to Poznań *(see next page)* from Biskupin either take the E261 via Gniezno or, if you have a good map, follow the minor road that leads to the city through attractive villages.

Biskupin open-air museum

ŁAGÓW

A wide road leads west from Poznań in the direction of the German border, reaching the town of **Świebodzin** after 122km (76 miles). To appreciate the charms of this part of Poland, a stop at ★ **Łagów** (pop. 6,000; 468km/292 miles) is recommended. This classic resort among beech forests is splendidly located between Lake Lagowskie and Lake Ciecz, and is popular with holidaymakers. The tower of the **castle** (zamek), built by the Knights of St John, is visible from afar; dating from the 14th century it is surrounded by forbidding defensive walls. A small hotel is located in the castle.

7: Poznań

The commercial centre and trade fair city of
★★ **Poznań** (pop. 600,000) is the most important
city in western Poland after Warsaw, from an economic, cultural and historical point of view. The
area around Poznań, Wielkopolska (Greater
Poland), is regarded as the heart of the Polish state.

History

Astride the legendary Amber Route between the
Baltic coast and the Mediterranean, Poznań's
favourable position on the River Warta was responsible for its development as a trading centre. This
tradition dates back to the 15th century, when several business-minded citizens got together and
organised the first official trade fair; this event soon
became so well-known that its fame spread even
to the Far East.

Poznań has had to endure turbulent periods during its
long history trying to maintain its reputation as a key
political and cultural centre; this strength was sometimes concealed by its popular image as a city of shop-
keepers. In the 19th-century partition of Poland the
city became part of the Prussian state and Prussian char-
acteristics came to be attributed to the Polish citizens
of Poznań; they were thus said to be efficient and reli-
able but not very hospitable and lacking in imagination.

Star Attraction
● Poznań

*Below and bottom: Poznań
market square*

Map below

However, their patriotism was never in question, and the city played a major part in the Polish independence movement, which was repeated later in the struggle against the Nazis. During World War II, nearly half the city was destroyed, but reconstruction proceeded rapidly and re-established the city's great appeal, while the pre-war population figures were quickly doubled.

Literary heritage

Poznań's Old Market Square encompasses an amazing range of museums, including the Henryk Sienkiewicz Literary Museum (Muzeum Literackie Henryka Sienkiewicza) at No. 84. As one of Poland's most eminent authors, Henryk Sienkiewicz won the Nobel Prize for Literature in 1905 with his epic *Quo Vadis*, set in ancient Rome, which became an international phenomenon. Arranged like a private residence, the museum has plenty of Sienkiewicz memorabilia and authentic interiors. This makes for a fascinating period piece, evoking early 20th-century literary life. Open Mon–Fri 10am–5pm.

SIGHTS

Leaving the exhibition centre to the west of the city centre and entering the historic heart of Poznań, you first encounter the **Monument to the Victims of June 1956 ❶**, a reminder of recent history when the workers went on strike in protest against the Communist government. Opposite the monument is the massive grey bulk of the **Palace of Culture ❷** (Pałac Kultury), the former residence of Wilhelm II in a palatial neo-Romanesque style. In spite of its rather off-putting appearance, it is worth investigating as it almost always has interesting exhibitions.

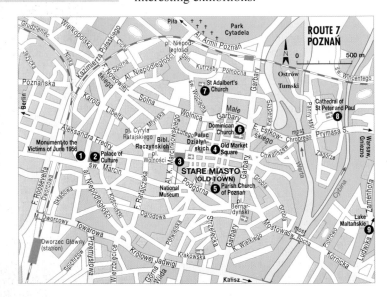

DOWNTOWN POZNAŃ

The main shopping street, Św Marcin (St Martin's), has all the atmosphere of a lively, modern big city. From here art lovers can head towards the ★ **National Museum ❸** (Muzeum Narodowe; open Tues 10am–6pm, Wed 9am–5pm, Thur 10am–4pm, Fri–Sat 10am–5pm, Sun 10am–3pm). Its comprehensive collections cover ethnography, city history and arts and crafts, but the collection most worth seeing comprises paintings by Polish and other European old masters, including works by Ribera, Zurbarán, Bellini and Bronzino.

Diagonally opposite, on the Plac Wolności, is the imposing 1829 **Raczyński Library** (Biblioteka Raczyńskich) with a magnificent neoclassical facade featuring 24 Corinthian columns. The library is a monument to the coexistence of the Poles and Germans at the beginning of the 19th century, which came to an end in the following decades with the growing insistence on Germanisation.

THE OLD TOWN

Continuing into the Old Town you pass the **Działyński Palace**, a 1773 burgher's house that is an unusual mixture of late baroque and neoclassical styles, before arriving at the delightful ★ **Old Market Square ❹** (Stary Rynek). The finest building here is the ★★ **Town Hall** (Ratusz), an excellent example of secular Polish-Italian architecture. It was rebuilt in the 16th century, when it acquired its present elegant, Renaissance form. Its most striking feature is the complex main facade, embellished with sgraffito, which consists of three floors of arcaded loggias topped by a high attic. Inside is the **Historical Museum of Poznań** (Muzeum Historii Miasta Poznania; open Tues, Thurs, Fri 9am–4pm, Wed 11am–6pm, Sat 10am–4pm, Sun 10am–3pm). Perhaps even more interesting than the exhibits, however, are the Renaissance rooms with original interiors, including the splendid Great Hall featuring a coffered ceiling that rests on only two pillars.

Przemysła Castle (Zamek Przemysła) is an atmospheric setting for the **Museum of**

Star Attraction
● Town Hall

Poznań Town Hall

Maps on pages 72, 66–7

Musical history

Another of Poznań's unusual museums is the Musical Instruments Museum (Muzeum Instrumentów Muzycznych) at No. 45 in the Old Market Square. Set in a grand burgher's house, the range of instruments is amazing. One room has a collection of pianos, each of which was played by Frederic Chopin, Poland's pre-eminent composer. Open Tues–Sat 11am–5pm, Sun 10am–3pm.

Decorative Arts (Muzeum Rzemiosł Artystycznych; open Tues–Sat 10am–4pm, Sun 10am–3pm), which has a fascinating collection. Ranging from Gothic and Renaissance to Art Deco, this includes silver, gold, glassware, porcelain and objets d'art.

The **Archaeological Museum** (Muzeum Archeologiczne; open Tues–Fri 10am–4pm, Sat 10am–6pm, Sun 10am–3pm) near the Old Market Square (ulica Wodna 27) has finds from the Stone Age to the late Middle Ages. It is the second oldest museum in Poland and is housed in the excellently restored Gorków Palace. Close to the museum, in ulica Gołębia, is the ★ **Parish Church of Poznań** ❺ (Kośćiół Farny), built by the Jesuits in the second half of the 17th century. Massive pillars which, in accordance with the illusionistic style of the baroque era have no supporting function, dominate the interior of the church.

CHURCHES

Of the numerous other churches in the city, the **Dominican Church** ❻ (Kośćiół Dominikanów) in ulica Dominikańska is particularly worth a visit. Although it was rebuilt in the baroque style, the church still has a fine brick portal dating from the 13th century. It was the Dominicans who brought the techniques of Gothic brick architecture

The Parish Church of Poznań

from Italy to Poland before the German Gothic style took over in Pomerania and in Prussia, where the order originated.

It is worth taking the trouble to visit **St Adalbert's Church** ❼ (Kośćiół Św Wojciecha) a little further out of the centre. Perched on a hill and readily identified by its wooden bell tower, it may not look very special, but is important to the citizens of Poznań, primarily as the burial place of many renowned people, including Józef Wybicki (1747–1822), the composer of the Polish national anthem.

Star Attraction
● **Cathedral of SS Peter and Paul**

THE CATHEDRAL

Now cross the Warta river to the ★★ **Cathedral of SS Peter and Paul** ❽ (Katedra Św Piotra i Pawła). Set on Cathedral Island (Ostrów Tumski), no longer exactly an island since the arm of the river has gradually narrowed, this is the location of several historic buildings. The cathedral is virtually a Polish national shrine, since this is the burial place of the nation's founder, Mieszko I. His mausoleum and that of his successor, Bolesław Chrobry I, are within the **Golden Chapel**, a 19th-century addition in neo-Byzantine style. As the cathedral was continually extended and refurbished during its long history, the architecture includes various styles: Romanesque, Gothic, Renaissance, baroque and neoclassical. Next to the cathedral is the medieval **Church of the Blessed Virgin Mary** (Kośćiół NMP), and the **Bishop's Palace** (Pałac Biskupów).

After so much culture you may well be ready for a break, and this last stop on your tour of the city is conveniently close to **Lake Maltańskie** ❾, where welcome refreshments are waiting in cafés and beer gardens. There are various walking trails around this vast lake, and rowing and canoeing regattas are often held here.

Cathedral of SS Peter and Paul

EXCURSIONS

Instead of heading west out of Poznań straight away *(see page 70)*, it is worth spending a day visiting the area to the south of the city.

Map
on pages
66–67

Architectural delight

In the village of Antonin, east of Poznań and south of Kalisz, set amidst dense forests, is the palatial hunting lodge of Antonin. While Poland has a wide range of important historic wooden architecture, including churches and manor houses, this neoclassical building is undoubtedly the grandest. Built in 1824, for aristocrat Antoni Radziwił, it was designed by the distinguished architect Karl Friedrich Schinkel.

Rogalin Palace chapel

KÓRNIK

Kórnik (pop. 8,000) is just 20km (12 miles) away and the first thing you see on arrival is the palace, which has an idyllic location on the shore of Kórnickie Lake. ★ **Kórnik Palace** originates from the late 14th century. However, in the first half of the 19th century it was redesigned in the English neo-Gothic style, a project in which the German architect Karl Friedrich Schinkel was involved. The palace has retained Romanesque fragments and a medieval moat.

The adjoining arboretum, influenced by English landscape gardening traditions, is an extensive park containing more than 3,000 species of exotic trees from all over the world. The eclectic museum collection includes every kind of object that one might expect to find: furniture, paintings, porcelain, silverware, armour, oriental weapons and objets d'art.

ROGALIN

Some 13km (8 miles) further on, the village of Rogalin on the River Warta also has a beautiful park with another prestigious residence built by Polish aristocrats. The ★ **Rogalin Palace** was owned by the Raczynski family and is a distinguished combination of rococo and neoclassical architecture. Open to the public, it has an interesting collection of clocks, together with furniture and various objets d'art. A gallery exhibiting excellent 19th- and 20th-century Polish and Western European paintings and a fine collection of old coaches are accommodated in pavilions adjacent to the palace.

While the aristocrats of Kórnik were influenced by English garden traditions, the owners of Rogalin favoured the French style. The park merges with an oak forest with impressive claims to fame; it has the greatest number of oak trees of any forest in Europe. This includes more than 1,000 trees known as the Rogalin Oaks. The park itself contains three oak trees which are 800 years old – the oldest and largest in Europe. They have been named after the three founders of the Slavic nations – Lech (Poland), Czech (Bohemia) and Rus (Russia).

8: The Southeast

Warsaw – Kazimierz Dolny – Lublin – Zamość – Przemyśl – Zakopane – High Tatras (786km/ 49 miles)

Map on pages 66–7

This route, which travels down from the capital into the southeast of the country, is full of fascinating sights and contrasts. Unspoilt nature, solitude and wilderness alternate with the outstanding historic architecture of old towns such as Zamość and Łańcut.

In order to be sure of accommodation during the peak summer season in this region it is best to make reservations in advance. This tour can be equally attractive in summer and winter and takes approximately 10 days. Although there are good rail and coach links, a car is the best form of transport, especially when touring in the mountains.

Below: the Przybylow House, Kazimierz Dolny
Bottom: castle walls and Vistula river, Kazimierz Dolny

RIVER VIEW

Leaving Warsaw in the direction of Dębin, following the road along the east bank of the River Vistula, you will be rewarded with a stretch of fine scenery along the river on your way to **Puławy**. In the middle of this industrial town is the romantic park of the Czartoryski family: the 'Gothic House' in this park is one of Poland's earliest public museums.

Map on pages 66–67

Below and bottom: Colourful landscapes near Lublin

KAZIMIERZ DOLNY

It is now only 14km (9 miles) to ★★ **Kazimierz Dolny** (pop. 5,000; 136km/85 miles). Described without exaggeration as one of the most beautiful places in Poland and set within an extensive national park, the town has captivated generations of artists with its bohemian and artistic flair. The Old Town, with a picturesque market square, is a particular attraction which has been immortalised on canvas hundreds of times.

The ornamental, late Renaissance and Mannerist facades of the burghers' houses that face on to the market square testify to the prosperity of the grain merchants who established the wealth of the town. The **parish church** (Kościół Farny), which stands at a slight incline above the market square, is an example of the Lublin Renaissance style, characterised by the particularly elaborate stuccowork with which the vault is decorated. Its organ, dating from 1620, is renowned throughout the country for its beauty and quality.

Dominating the town is the 14th-century ruin of the **Royal Castle** and the adjacent watchtower. Among the town's other historic buildings are various wooden houses traditionally inhabited by artists and writers, and 16th- and 17th-century granaries overlooking the river.

LUBLIN

★ **Lublin** (pop. 350,000; 187km/117 miles) could not be more of a contrast, either from the point of view of size or atmosphere. This otherwise provincial town is considerably enlivened by the presence of two universities, the Catholic and the State University of Lublin, and the population is also swelled by numerous travelling salesmen from the neighbouring countries on Poland's eastern border.

The historic Old Town in the city centre is dominated by the ★ **castle**. The most important building in this complex is the Gothic **Castle Cathedral**. Its interior is entirely decorated with wall paintings in the Ruthenian/Byzantine style, which in the austere Gothic surroundings seem positively exotic.

Today the primarily neo-Gothic castle complex houses a museum of Polish painting, folk art and archaeology (open Wed–Sat 9am–4pm, Sun 9am–5pm, closed Mon).

The medieval city centre lies at the foot of the castle. To the west are remains of the former city wall, dating from the 14th century and including the Cracow Gate (Brama Krakowska). Like many of the buildings in the Old Town, the **cathedral** is a mixture of styles. The facade, rebuilt in 1819, is neoclassical, while the interior is baroque. The neighbouring Dominican church was originally built in the Gothic style, but several interesting domed chapels in late Renaissance style have since been added.

Star Attraction
● Kazimierz Dolny
● Zamość

ZAMOŚĆ

The small Renaissance town of ★★ **Zamość** (pop. 55,000; 272km/170 miles) is an architectural gem. In no other town in Poland or Western Europe – with the exception of Italy, the home of the Renaissance – has this building style been so perfectly preserved. In 1580 the Polish chancellor Jan Zamoyski commissioned the Venetian architect Bernardo Morando to design a whole town here in the middle of the countryside: the result was this classic example of European civic architecture in the Renaissance period.

A beautiful setting
In addition to the historic beauty of Kazimierz Dolny's architecture, the immediate area surrounding the town offers many fine buildings, not to mention the natural beauty of the landscape. Views across the River Vistula are idyllic, as is the surrounding wooded countryside; while the romantic views include a ruined castle.

Zamość market square

Map on pages 66–67

Belwo: Zamość Town Hall
Bottom: Łańcut palace

TOWN HALL

The ★★ **Town Hall** (Ratusz), with a 50-m (165-ft) octagonal tower, crowned with a baroque helmet, dominates the Great Market Square. The double staircase was added to this late Renaissance building in the 18th century and reflects the theatricality of the baroque style. It blends in so well, however, that many visitors are astonished to learn that it was built much later.

The square is lined with the most beautiful burghers' houses connected by arcaded passages. Southwest of the square, the Collegiate Church, richly decorated with sculptures and stuccowork, is a further example of Bernardo Morando's artistry.

Zamość can still be admired in all its former glory today as it was spared destruction during World War II. The Nazis had quite different plans for it: the Polish citizens were to be expelled and the town was to become a 'German outpost' renamed 'Himmlerstadt' and repopulated with ethnic Germans.

ŁAŃCUT

The road to **Łańcut** (pop. 16,000; 409km/256 miles) illustrates just how sparsely populated this southeastern part of Poland is. The town of Łańcut is the location of one of the most magnificent aristocratic residences in Poland; the early baroque ★ **palace** in the eastern part of the town was built in 1629–41 and has more than 300 rooms. It is now a museum of interior design. The palace is set in an extensive park with an orangery, stable block and various other outbuildings.

The **Carriage Museum** (both museums open Tues–Sat 9am–3pm, Sun 9am–4pm, June–Sept Sat–Sun 10am–5pm, closed Dec, Jan, closed Mon) in the southern part of the palace park is said to be the largest collection of its kind in Europe, with more than 50 exhibits.

PRZEMYŚL

From Łańcut proceed to ★ **Przemyśl** (pop. 65,000; 476km/298 miles) on the River San, which is characterised by monumental architecture. On top of the hill is the ★ **Royal Castle** (Zamek Kró-lewski) built by Kazimierz the Great in the 14th century, and later reconstructed in the Renaissance style. The foundation stone for the original Gothic cathedral was laid in 1460, and in 1724–44 this was rebuilt in the baroque style. Various other churches and monastic complexes span a range of architectural styles. In World War I the fortress of Przemyśl played a key part in the confrontations between Russia and Austria-Hungary.

The village of **Krasiczyn**, 10km (6 miles) to the west, has a famous ★ **palace** worth seeing. This impressive Renaissance building was commissioned by the Krasicki family in 1580; its most outstanding features are its four towers, each individually designed, and the facade, with its sgraffito decorations. The palace, which is now run as a luxury hotel, is surrounded by a splendid park.

PANORAMIC BEAUTY

Krasiczyn marks the start of the most beautiful stretch of this route, the road winding through magnificent mountain scenery with panoramic views of green valleys. Your first destination is **Sanok** (pop. 35,000; 548km/343 miles). This town is an ideal starting point for excursions in the Bieszczady, a range of mountains forming part of the Carpathians. There is an interesting

Star Attraction
● **Zamość Town Hall**

Around Łancut
Two interesting towns within easy reach of Łancut are Rzeszów and Kolbuszowo. Founded in 1354, Rzeszów offers a range of historic buildings, including a 17th-century Bernardine monastic complex, and the former Piarist monastery, which now houses the regional museum. The town hall is 18th century. Kolbuszowo has a *skansen* museum of traditional regional building styles.

Spectacular views near Zakopane

Map
on pages
66–7

collection of icons in the **Palace of Sanok** high up on the banks of the San, and the open-air museum *(skansen)* with examples of the architecture of the Lemks and Boyks, the two Ukrainian groups who lived in this area, is also well worth a visit.

LESKO

Below: Pieniny National Park
Bottom: Dunajec raftsmen

Lesko, just 13km (8 miles) from Sanok, marks the beginning (or end) of the Bieszczady loop road, a 160-km (100-mile) route through the beautiful scenery of the southeast tip of Poland. Those with hiking boots in their luggage will want to set out on foot, as there are some splendid trails through this unspoilt mountain region. If you have a tent and a little more time to spare, it is worth staying here for a few days to explore the countryside more thoroughly. In 1973 the outer edge of the Polish Carpathians was established as the ★**Bieszczady National Park**. The highest peak, the Tarnica (1,346m/4,416ft), is located here and the unspoilt conifer and beech woods are still inhabited by wolves, lynxes and brown bears.

CONTINUING VIA NOWY SĄCZ

From Sanok, continue via Krosno and the attractive little town of Biecz to **Nowy Sącz** (pop. 73,000; 688km/430 miles). Although it has several build-

ings of architectural interest, including the parish church, Franciscan church and an open-air museum, most tourists come here in search of nature, en route to the ★ **Pieniny National Park**, which is soon reached on the good road from Nowy Sącz. With an area of less than 3,000 hectares (7,400 acres), it is one of the smallest of the Polish national parks, but makes up for its lack of size in scenic beauty and an enormous variety of plant species.

The high point of a visit to this park – in fact, one of the most popular tourist attractions in Poland – is a ★★ **raft trip** on the Dunajec. The long rafts (departing from the Katy quay at Sromowce) are steered by the local Highlanders. Cutting through the Pieniny Mountains near the Slovakian border, the river forms a gorge almost 15km (9 miles) long between walls of rock 300m (980ft) high, and makes for an unforgettable experience. The raft trip ends in Szczawnica.

NOWY TARG

Nowy Targ (pop. 28,000; 765km/478 miles) is an industrial centre with some historic buildings; a key tourist attraction is market day. This is held each Thursday, when there is everything to be had, from Tatra sheepdogs to horses and wooden toys to cowbells. The village of **Dębno** is nearby, renowned for its beautifully preserved church; ★★ **St Michael the Archangel** is one of the most important buildings in Poland. Unlike anything that has been seen up to now, this church is made entirely of larchwood panels joined with wooden pins: there is not one metal nail in the building. The interior is covered with beautiful, late-Gothic stencil painting.

The wooden architecture in many of the small mountain villages of this region is the most striking example of the culture of the Highlanders (Górals), a strong ethnic group in Poland whose traditions, including their dialect and costumes, are still very much part of their everyday life. That the Górals were able to build so many fine houses is paradoxically due to their former poverty; many left the country to seek their fortune in the United States and, in accordance with tradition, the

Star Attractions
● **River rafting**
● **Church of St Michael the Archangel**

Mountain peaks
Southeastern Poland offers some of the most beautiful mountain ranges, including the Pieniny, the Beskid Sądecki, Beskid Niski and Bieszczady. This 'green belt' is a haven of unusual and unique flora and fauna. The resort of Krościenko, at the foot of the Pieniny Mountains, is a good base from which to explore.

Zakopane traditional architecture

Map on pages 66–67

Zakopane
The future of Zakopane changed dramatically after being visited by Dr Chałubiński from Warsaw. He began to spread the word of the immense charm and beauty of this Góral (Highlanders') sheep farming village, and from the 1870s a growing number of Polish intellectuals and artists began to settle here. Zakopane soon became a cultural and political centre. Museums detail the lives and works of some of the most celebrated residents, including the composer Karol Szymanowski.

Morskie Oko in the Tatras

emigrés supported the relatives they had left behind. Today most Highlanders make their money letting rooms to tourists, but some still earn their living as sheep farmers, producing two popular, traditional cheeses, *bryndza* and *oscypek*.

★ **Zakopane** (pop. 33,000) is the gateway to one of Poland's greatest natural treasures, the Tatra mountain chain; it is a winter sports centre with good ski slopes, several ski jumps and more than 50 ski lifts. What was once a highland village has now become a very popular destination all year round, but it manages to retain its original village atmosphere. In many of the smaller places surrounding Zakopane, it is easy to enjoy the peace and quiet of the mountains.

The **Tatra Museum** (Muzeum Tatrzańskie, open Tues–Sat 9am–5pm, Sun 9am–3pm) in Zakopane includes exhibits relating to the traditional customs of the Highlanders and a natural history collection. Historic wooden houses and churches in the distinctive local Zakopane style can be seen throughout the town. Accommodation is available in a number of comfortable hotels, youth hostels, mountain huts and guesthouses.

THE TATRAS

The entire ★★ **Tatra Mountains** region has been established as two national parks, one on the Polish side of the border and the other in Slovakia. With peaks of more than 2,000m (6,500ft), this enchanting mountain range is the home of rare species such as golden eagles, marmots, chamois and lynxes. In this alpine scenery, with its abundance of streams, waterfalls and lakes, there are numerous beautiful spots to visit and an assortment of trails, ranging from a gentle stroll to a climb. The paths are well marked and mountain climbing in the Tatras is greatly facilitated by the professional services of the local guides. The famous mountain lake ★ **Morskie Oko** (literally 'eye of the sea') is the most popular beauty spot. Splendidly located at a height of 1,400m (4,590ft), this 35-hectare (86-acre) lake is easily accessible.

9: Cracow

The former capital of Poland, Cracow (Kraków) has retained its status as the country's intellectual and artistic centre. This accounts for the extraordinary atmosphere: Bohemian, flamboyant, relaxed and friendly, though inevitably there is also a sense of elitism (the city's university thrives on the same status as Oxford or Cambridge). Twice a European City of Culture, most recently in 2000, it is immediately apparent why.

Virtually the entire city centre is pedestrianised, which simplifies getting around, and it's compact enough to be easily navigable, while comprehensive enough to have numerous buildings in different architectural styles. These include Romanesque, Gothic, Renaissance (with Italianate Renaissance adding variety), baroque, rococo, neoclassical, Secessionist (central and eastern European Art Nouveau) and Art Deco. Consequently, you can see plenty of amazing sights just wandering around, but there is so much to see that it is worth following itineraries to ensure you don't miss the best.

Cracow's churches provide an extraordinary chronicle of sacral art, architecture, and the various saints with special status in Poland. In the district of Kazimierz, historically inhabited by the Jewish community, several synagogues can also be visited.

In addition to the National Museum and Wawel

Map on page 86

Star Attraction
● **Tatra Mountains**

Below: on Floriańska Street
Bottom: Café Noworolski in the arcade of the Sukiennice

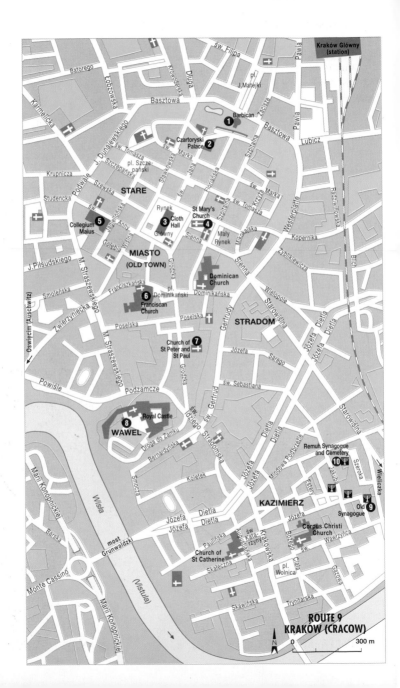

ROUTE 9
KRAKÓW (CRACOW)

Royal Castle, Cracow has an amazing range of museums, housed within period buildings rather than 'purpose-built' settings. The Czartoryski Museum, for example, is in a former palace and monastery, while the homes of painters Jan Matejko and Józef Mehoffer are 'museum homes' detailing their lives and works.

At the centre of Cracow life is the Old Town market square. It has a wonderful, colourful character, with numerous flower stalls, Cracovian folk musicians playing popular refrains and the statue of Adam Mickiewicz, Poland's premier romantic poet, which is a popular meeting place. You're never far from a café, so having a break in one of a variety of settings is never hard. The entire Old Town is encircled by a series of delightful gardens, which are an ideal route to take when walking to destinations in different parts of the city, or just to enjoy in their own right.

Map opposite

Festival city

In addition to all the permanent attractions, Cracow has a range of fascinating annual events, held throughout the year to commemorate specific feast days and holidays. The city also has a large number of annual festivals, covering music, opera, film, the visual arts, theatre and folk arts and crafts, such as the Christmas Nativity Crib competition in December.

HISTORY

With such a distinguished history, Cracow has various key dates. The 9th-century AD fortified settlement established on Wawel Hill was the earliest seat of the Wiślan (Vistulan) dukes. This evolved into an important centre in the early 11th century, when the diocese of Cracow was established, and the first cathedral was constructed here. When Cracow became the capital of Poland in 1038, King Kazimierz Odnowiciel (Casimir the Restorer) established the first royal residence on Wawel Hill. Meanwhile, Cracow's strategic location linking the east with Western Europe and Scandinavia had ensured its position as an important trading centre. Gaining municipal status in 1257, the Jagiellon University of Cracow was founded in 1364, the first in the country and the second in Central Europe after the University of Prague.

After Warsaw was proclaimed the capital in 1596 the city lost its political importance, but it continued as the cultural capital of Poland. During the partitions of Poland (1793–1918), Cracow came under the rule of the Austro-Hungarian Empire. Towards the end of World War II, Cracow was scheduled

Main Market Square

Map on page 86

Below: Café Huśtawka sign
Bottom: inside Café Larousse

for destruction by the Nazis. By a stroke of good fortune, the city managed to avoid the fate of Warsaw and survived the war unharmed. A new threat, however, was already on the way. In the 1950s the huge steelworks of Nowa Huta were built on the edge of the city, with the idea of introducing a 'proletarian element', represented by the 30,000 steelworkers, to counterbalance Cracow's intellectual elite and impose the socialist spirit on the city. Nowa Huta had a disastrous effect on the priceless historical monuments of Cracow, compounded by the pollution from the industry of Upper Silesia. Fortunately, tough ecological regulations have countered this, and extensive restoration has preserved the city's beauty.

The centre has remained largely unchanged since the Middle Ages. The defensive walls were left standing until the 19th century, when they were demolished to create a green belt, the Planty Park, which surrounds the entire centre.

THE OLD TOWN

With most of the ★★★ **Old Town** pedestrianised, walking is the best – indeed the only – way to sightsee (apart from horse-drawn carriages). The 15th-century ★ **Barbican ❶** (Barbakan; open daily 10.30am–6pm May–Oct), is a circular defensive bastion in front of ★ **Florian's Gate** (Brama Florianska), which leads to the centre. It is the only remaining gate which, together with adjoining sections of the original city wall and fortified towers, dates from the 13th and 14th centuries. Today, artists use the walls as an open-air gallery for their work, with everything on offer from views of the city to gypsy women. Continue to the **Czartoryski Museum ❷** (Muzeum Czartoryskich; open Tues, Thur, Sat–Sun 10am–3.30pm, Wed, Fri 10am–6pm), which houses a fine collection of Italian, German and Dutch masters, including the world-famous painting *Lady with an Ermine* by Leonardo da Vinci.

Florian's Street (ulica Floriańska), leading into the centre of the Old Town from Florian's gate, is a popular place to stroll. Before following the stream of tourists and residents to the main market square (Rynek Główny), however, pay a visit to the historic Bohemian café Jama Michalikowa at No. 45, and enjoy a coffee in the flamboyant atmosphere provided by the Viennese Secessionist surroundings. Even in Vienna itself it would be hard to find its equal.

Star Attractions
● **Cracow Old Town**
● **Main Market Square**

MARKET SQUARE

Fortified by refreshments, continue on to the extensive ★★ **Main Market Square** (Rynek Główny) in the heart of Cracow. Of all the medieval market squares in Europe, only St Mark's Square in Venice is larger. Numerous flower stalls provide plenty of colour, and traditional bread rings are sold from glass carts. People fill the surrounding cafés (the tables are placed outside with the first rays of morning sun) or stand around in small groups discussing the day's news. At the centre of the square is the ★ **Cloth Hall** ❸ (Sukiennice), which still fulfils its original function as a trading centre, being an elegant shopping arcade.

The building actually dates from the 14th century, but was so beautifully rebuilt during the Renaissance era that it became a source of inspiration to many architects elsewhere. The most frequently copied aspect was the elaborate attic, which conceals a steep roof, with the retaining wall richly

Exploring the square
The main market square is lined with imposing burghers' houses and palaces, surrounding the Town Hall Tower (which can be visited). This is all that remains of the original town hall. On another corner is the diminutive church of St Adalbert, which has retained many of its original Romanesque features, and a beautiful baroque altar.

The Cloth Hall

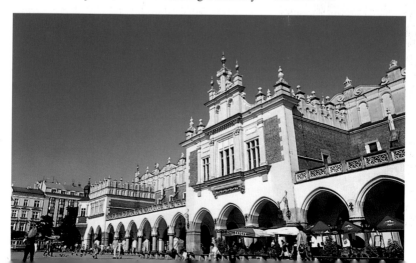

Map
on page
86

Astronomical achievements

After completing his studies at Collegium Maius in 1491–5, Nicolas Copernicus (Mikołaj Kopernik) gradually developed a theory that changed the founding principle of astronomy. In 1530 he published a theory stating that the sun, and not the earth, was the centre of the universe, and that the planets actually revolved around the sun. However, the initial reaction was not positive; in fact, it was condemned by the Roman Catholic Church as heresy.

ornamented with masked heads. The **Gallery of 19th-Century Polish Painting and Sculpture** (Galeria Sztuki Polskiej XIX Wieku; open Tues, Fri, Sat 10am–7pm, Wed, Thurs 10am–4pm, Sun 10am–3pm) is on the upper floors of the Cloth Hall.

St Mary's Church

The Rynek Główny is lined with burghers' houses that exemplify various architectural styles. This includes Dom Hipolytów, at pl Mariacki 3, a 17th century merchant's house which is a museum. The east corner of the square features the imposing ★ **St Mary's Church** ❹ (Kościół Mariacki). A Gothic 14th-century basilica with three aisles, its two individually designed towers are a distinctive feature. Every hour, the famous trumpet fanfare, which historically warned the city of impending attacks, is played live from the left-hand tower.

The ornate, intricate interiors include Gothic, Renaissance and baroque elements. The famous ★★ **main altar** of St Mary's is a masterpiece of late Gothic carving. Veit Stoss of Nuremberg (or Wit Stwosz, as he was known to the Poles) was summoned to Cracow for this purpose, completing the triptych altarpiece in 1489. Standing 13 metres (43ft) high, it is the largest medieval altar in existence. Stoss was held in such high esteem in the then Polish capital that he remained for almost 20

St Mary's Church

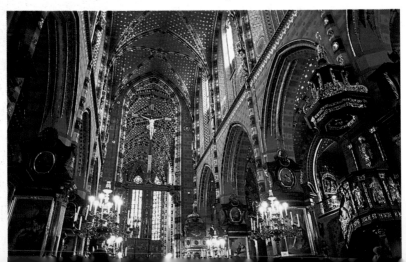

years, completing several works for the Polish nobility and the king. The altar depicts numerous Biblical scenes, while the central panel is an impressive and dramatic representation of the death of the Virgin Mary, surrounded by the Apostles.

★

Star Attractions
● Altar of St Mary's Church
● Wawel Hill

ACADEMIC CRACOW

From the market proceed to the earliest college of Cracow University, the ★ **Collegium Maius ❺**. There is a beautiful Gothic arcaded courtyard, with the University Museum (Mon–Fri 10am– 2.20pm, Sat 10am–1.20pm) housed in the original professors' quarters. This includes memorabilia of the institution's most famous students, including the astronomer Nicolas Copernicus.

Below: Collegiun Maius courtyard
Bottom: Wawel Cathedral

Return to the market and follow the ulica Grodzka in the direction of the Wawel Castle to reach the ★ **Franciscan Church ❻** (Kościół Franczyszkanów), with its fascinating combination of styles. The Gothic interior is decorated with Secessionist stained-glass windows by the Polish turn-of-the-20th-century genius, Stanisław Wyspiański, an artist and dramatist who belonged to a movement called Young Poland (Młoda Polska). Continuing to Wawel Hill, take a look at the ★ **Church of St Peter and St Paul ❼** (Kościół Św Piotra i Pawła), one of the finest baroque churches in Poland. The architect modelled this masterwork, built for the Jesuits, on their church, Il Gesù, in Rome – the result is magnificent.

WAWEL HILL

The distinguished series of buildings that comprise ★★★ **Wawel Hill ❽** combine a variety of styles to form a harmonious complex. The **Wawel Cathedral** (Katedra Wawelska; open Mon–Sat 9am– 5pm, Sun 12.15–5pm Apr–Sept, otherwise usually closes 4pm or 3pm Nov–March) is important not only as a religious building, but also for the part it has played in the nation's history. From 1320, this was the place where Polish kings were crowned and buried in the crypt, together with religious leaders, statesmen and cultural figures such as the poet

Maps
on pages
86, 66–7

Adam Mickiewicz. The interiors combine Gothic, Renaissance, baroque and neoclassical elements. There are 18 side chapels, including the **Holy Cross Chapel** (Kaplica Świętokrzyska) with Ruthenian and Byzantine frescoes, and the marble sarcophagus of the Jagiellonian king Kazimierz IV by Veit Stoss. The superb Renaissance **Sigismund Chapel** (Kaplica Zygmuntowska) has a gilded dome.

*Below: a Jewish sign
in Kazimierz
Bottom: the Envoy's Hall,
Wawel Castle*

ROYAL CASTLE

The ★★**Wawel Castle** is a magnificent building that was the residence of Polish kings for centuries, and the distinguished architecture is embellished with numerous impressive works of art. The present exterior dates back to 1502–36 when the castle was rebuilt in the Renaissance style. The arcaded courtyard is also from this period: elegant and harmoniously proportioned, it is one of the most outstanding examples of its kind in Europe. The ★**Royal Apartments** (open Mon 9.30am– noon, Tues, Fri 9.30am–4pm, Wed, Thur, Sat 9.30am–3pm, Sun 10am–3pm) cover a huge range of exhibits: furniture, paintings, sculptures and objets d'art. The most valuable items are the 142 tapestries made in Brussels for the last Jagiellonian king, Zygmunt August. Other museums in the Wawel complex include the Royal Treasury and Armoury, and the Lost Wawel, with archaeological exhibits.

KAZIMIERZ

Kazimierz was founded as a separate town in 1335 by King Casimir the Great (Kazimierz Wielki). From 1495 a large Jewish population was established here, arriving from all over Europe. Kazimierz became a part of Cracow in 1800. In 1941 the Nazis first confined the Jewish population to a ghetto in another part of Cracow, before sending them to Auschwitz.

SYNAGOGUE AND CEMETERY

The Jewish Museum in the former ★ **Old Synagogue ❾** (Stara Synagoga; open Mon 10am–2pm, Tues–Sun 10am–5pm) details the history of the Jewish culture that once flourished here. The nearby **Remuh Synagogue and Cemetery ❿**, named after a famous rabbi, date from the 1550s. This is one of only two remaining Renaissance Jewish cemeteries in Europe (the other is in Prague). The Jewish buildings of Kazimierz escaped destruction by the Nazis, who intended to set up a museum of 'vanished races' here.

Of the 68,000 Jewish inhabitants of Kazimierz in 1938, only a few thousand survived the extermination camps: that these individuals were saved was due in no small part to the efforts of Oskar Schindler, whose part in the war was portrayed in Steven Spielberg's movie *Schindler's List*. There are also several Jewish restaurants and cafés, clustered along ulica Szeroka.

EXCURSIONS

Take the suburban railway or bus to Wieliczka about 20 km (13 miles) outside Cracow, to the ★★ **Wieliczka Salt Mine** (Kopalnia Soli Wieliczka; open daily 7.30am–7.30pm Apr–Oct, otherwise 8am–5pm). Dating from the 12th century, this is the country's oldest working salt mine and deservedly merits an entry on UNESCO's World Cultural Heritage list. An amazing sequence of chambers linked by passageways includes displays of historic mining equipment and sculptures created from salt. The Chapel of St Kinga is a highlight, with

Star Attractions
● Wawel Castle
● Wieliczka Salt Mine

Other synagogues
Kazimierz has several other synagogues spanning various architectural styles. The Isaac Synagogue, for example, has baroque interiors dating from the mid-17th century, the Tempel Synagogue was built in 1862 in a neo-Renaissance style, with ornate interiors. The Centre for Jewish Culture, ulica Meiselsa 17, and the travel agency at ulica Szeroka 2 are good sources of information.

Monument to the salt workers, Wieliczka

Map on pages 66–67

An imposing abbey

Following the River Vistula several kilometres/miles west from Cracow, you'll find the Benedictine Abbey of Tyniec, which is reflected in the river from its towering position high above on a limestone cliff. Extended and rebuilt many times after various enemy armies inflicted their devastating blows, it is a harmonious combination of Romanesque, Gothic and baroque, and a delightful setting for the organ festivals that are held here each summer.

The infamous gates to Auschwitz camp

an altar, chandeliers and sacral art all sculpted from salt. The deposits reach a depth of 315m (1,034ft) and the total length of the galleries, chambers and tunnels is more than 150km (90 miles).

AUSCHWITZ (OSWIĘCIM)

Situated more than 50km (32 miles) west of Cracow is an industrial town whose name, Auschwitz (Oświęcim), will always remain synonymous with the most horrific genocide in history. The memorial in the grounds of the Auschwitz concentration camp – where in 1995 the 50th anniversary of its liberation by the Russians was commemorated – and the second memorial in Birkenau (Brzezinka), the camp 4km (2½ miles) to the west, commemorate the 1.5 million people who died here as victims of the Nazis.

Established in April 1940, this was the largest extermination camp in Poland, which actually comprised two separate camps. 'Auschwitz I' was a slave-labour camp for political prisoners and members of the Resistance, mainly Poles and Germans, as well as Soviet prisoners of war. More than 100,000 people lost their lives here. But it was in Birkenau, or 'Auschwitz II', established in 1941, that the SS developed their huge extermination complex, where approximately 1.5 million people of Jewish origin, transported from all over Europe in cattle trucks, were gassed.

The most horrific period was in 1942, when up to 20,000 people were gassed each day. Before the camps were liberated by the Red Army in 1945, the Nazis began detonating some of the buildings and destroying documentary evidence. Both camps were preserved and established as the National Museum of Martyrology (open daily 8am–7pm June–Aug; until 6pm May, Sept; 5pm Apr, Oct; 4pm March, 1 Nov–15 Dec; 3pm 15 Dec–Feb).

Guides provide objective background information on the site, but nothing can diminish the horror of this industrial extermination factory, with its 'bathhouses', barracks and cremating ovens. For obvious reasons, children under 12 are not admitted.

10: Silesia

Cracow – Częstochowa – Opole –Wrocław – Karkonosze Mountains (511km/319 miles)

The highlight of this route to Poland's western border is the historic Silesian metropolis of Wrocław. Silesia's scenic beauty, traditional spas, hiking trails through the Sudety Mountains, and numerous museums with a comprehensive range of major art treasures are among the attractions that await you.

Poland's intense Catholicism can be experienced in one of the world's most important shrines for pilgrimages: Częstochowa. Those who want to enjoy the countryside as well as absorbing the culture should allow at least six days for this route. To climb the Snieżka or go for a longer hike in the Sudety requires a few days more. There are newly opened hotels and guesthouses at all the destinations on this route, so finding accommodation should not be a problem. Booking ahead, particularly during the peak summer season, is always a sensible precaution.

After the concentrated culture of Cracow, the ★★**Ojców National Park** (Ojcówski Park Narodowy), which begins only a few kilometres north of the city, is a welcome contrast. It is a landscape of extraordinary beauty, with limestone cliffs, deeply carved valleys and eccentric stone and cliff

Map on pages 66–7

Star Attraction
● Ojców National Park

Below: Jasna Góra monastery
Bottom: Jelenia Góra

Map on pages 66–7

Statue at Jasna Góra

formations shaped like clubs, needles, towers and gates. The symbol of the park, in fact, is the famous **Club of Hercules**, an unusual pillar of rock standing 25 metres (82ft) high by the side of the road. At the northern end of the park is Pieskowa Skała, which has a beautiful early-Renaissance castle, ★ **Pieskowa Skała Castle**, with an arcaded courtyard, museum (open Tues–Thurs 9am–3pm, Fri 9am–noon, Sat, Sun 10am–5pm), and adjoining restaurant.

By the time you enter Upper Silesia, if not before, you may be thinking back to the tranquillity of the Ojców National Park, especially when the Huta Katowice (near Dabrowa Gornicza) and the region's other industrial centres come into view.

CZĘSTOCHOWA

Częstochowa (pop. 250,000; 126km/79 miles) offers a complete contrast of a different kind. It is one of the most important shrines of the cult of the Virgin Mary for Roman Catholic pilgrims, who come every year to the baroque ★★ **Monastery of Jasna Góra** (open daily 5.30am–5pm). The object of veneration is the miraculous **Black Madonna**

(Czarna Madonna), a Byzantine icon of the Virgin Mary holding the infant Jesus, which dates from the Middle Ages. Like the Black Madonnas of Montserrat, Altötting and Guadalupe, the Częstochowa Madonna is steeped in legend. The face bears two cuts inflicted by a Pagan warlord, which apparently began to bleed.

The picture is a prime example of a particular style of Byzantine icon painting where dark colours were used. In no other country in the world has a single work of art had such religious, social and above all political significance. During the Swedish invasion in 1655, the Swedes mounted a heavy siege on the monastery, set on a hill, which by this time had evolved into a fortified monastic complex. A sudden withdrawal by the Swedes was attributed to the intervention of the Black Madonna. This had a monumental impact, and as a result the Poles were able to drive the Swedes out of the country. King Kazimierz ceremoniously laid down his crown before the icon of the Madonna and in 1717 She was officially declared 'Queen of Poland'.

Star Attraction
● **Jasna Góra Monastery**

A national cult
The enormous importance of the cult of the Virgin Mary in Poland is at its strongest in Częstochowa, though there are 'miraculous' paintings and figures of Our Lady Mary in various churches throughout Poland. These include the painting of Our Lady of Kalwarja, and a statue of Our Lady of Lourdes at the Church of the Missionary Priests, both in Cracow.

THE ICON

The icon, donated in 1384 by Duke Władysław of Opole, is regarded as being Poland's greatest religious relic. The monastery itself was founded by the Pauline order, to the west of the original town centre, in 1382. The complex is dominated by the Gothic ★ **monastery church**, dating from 1463, surrounded by bastions and monastic buildings.

The icon of the Black Madonna is located over a priceless early baroque altar made of ebony and silver. Normally the picture is covered by a cloth, but it is unveiled with great ceremony and can be seen daily 6am–1pm, 2pm–9.30pm.

Pilgrims and tourists queue to see the holy picture, which it is claimed has miraculously cured numerous people. **The Armoury Museum** (open daily 9am–5pm), with valuable relics, and an impressive **Knights' Hall** of the baroque monastery, should not be missed.

Jasna Góra church

Map
on pages
66–7, 99

OPOLE

The route continues to **Opole** (pop. 120,000; 224km/140 miles). Originally the site of a fort constructed by the Opole tribe, the town was founded in 1217 on the right bank of the River Odra. There are many reminders of its early history, including the huge tower of the Piast Castle.

The market square is dominated by a town hall, which has an Italianate feel. This is no coincidence, since it is a copy of the Palazzo Vecchio in Florence. The sacral buildings of Opole, however, are entirely Polish in character: the Gothic Cathedral of the Holy Cross, by the Odra, which dates back to the 15th century, and the Franciscan monastery and church from the mid-14th century. Both churches contain tombs of Piast dukes of Opole.

Don't leave without a visit to the **Opole Village Museum** outside the town, an open-air museum featuring historic wooden peasants' houses from the region (Tues–Sun 10am–6pm, 15 April–15 Oct, otherwise 9am–2pm).

A choice of castles

Being close to Poland's southern border, the area around Wrocław has a large number of castles designed to fend off hostile incursions. Among the prime examples of Renaissance architecture are the castles in Oleśnica, Czocha, and Głogówek. The Renaissance castle in Wojnowice is surrounded by Lake Lesniańskie, while the extensive remains of the original castle can be seen in Ząbkowice.

BRZEG

Brzeg (pop. 37,000; 267km/167 miles) has a magnificent ★ **castle** (open Wed 10am–5.30pm, Tues, Thur–Sun 10am–4.30pm) arranged round a courtyard with arcades on several floors. Built by the Slav dukes of the Piast dynasty, it is one of the most important Renaissance monuments in Poland and is thought to have been modelled on the Wawel Castle in Cracow.

Brzeg castle facade

WROCŁAW

★★ **Wrocław** (pop. 643,600; 309km/193 miles) evolved due to its ideal position on the Odra River in the centre of the Silesian lowlands, on the original trade route linking Western Europe with Russia. The city dates back to the 10th century when the island of Ostrów Tumski was settled. Later the Sleżanie built a castle here, and in the year 1000, the king of Poland founded one of the first dioceses here. Wrocław has changed nationality several times in its history. When Silesia was still the most important province in the former Polish Pi-ast state, Wrocław was the centre of the region. In 1335 it came under Bohemian rule, from 1526 it belonged to the Habsburgs, and in 1741 it was captured by the Prussians. After World War II, Wrocław became a Polish city again, following years as part of Germany, when it was known as Breslau. After the German population left, Wrocław was primarily resettled by displaced Poles from former Polish territory in the present-day Ukraine.

Star Attraction
● **Wrocław Town Hall**

SIGHTS

The Old Town features a spectacular range of archi-tectural styles, with the vast market square linked to two further squares. The ★★**Town Hall** ❶ (Ratusz; open Mon–Sat 11am–5pm, Sun 10am–6pm) is considered to be one of the finest Gothic

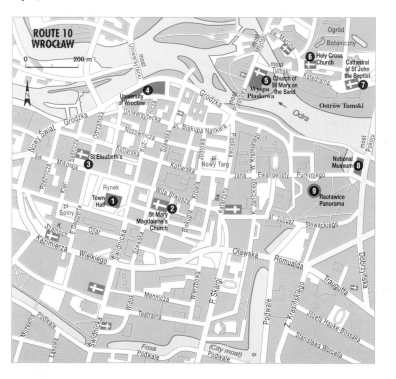

Map
on pages
66–7, 99

civic buildings in Europe, featuring an ornamental facade decorated with tracery. The interiors are equally impressive, with fine panelling, Renaissance painting and magnificent vaulting. The beer cellar dates from the 15th century.

Not far from the Town Hall is the red brick building of **St Mary Magdalene's Church ②** (Kościół Św Marii Magdaleny). This dates from the 14th century, and features, in an outer wall, a 12th-century Romanesque portal from a former Benedictine abbey. The tower of the Gothic church, **St Elizabeth's ③** (Kościół Św Elżbiety), is the highest in the city. North of the old town, by the Odra, are the buildings of the ★ **University of Wrocław ④**. In the Collegium Maximum, the main building constructed in 1728–41, is the assembly hall ★ ★ **Aula Leopoldina** (open Mon, Tues, Thur 10.30am–3.30pm, Fri–Sun 11am–5pm), without a doubt the most beautiful baroque hall in Poland, where frescoes and sculpture combine to perfection.

Below: Wrocław town hall astronomical clock
Bottom: Wrocław market square

AN HISTORIC ISLAND

Cross the bridge over the Odra River to Sand Island (Wyspa Piaskowa), dominated by the Gothic ★ **Church of St Mary on the Sand ⑤** (Kościół Św Panny na Piasku). The distinguishing features of the interiors are several late-Gothic altars and the stained-glass windows. A small bridge leads to

Ostrów Tumski (Cathedral Island), the original centre of Wrocław under the Slav dukes. The first church is the **Holy Cross Church** (Kościół Św Krzyża), an elegant Gothic building which, unusually, incorporates two churches. On the lower 'floor', which resembles a large crypt, is the Greek-Catholic (Uniate) Church of St Bartholomew's, and above it the Holy Cross Church.

Walk past the 18th-century archbishop's residence to the ★ **Cathedral of St John the Baptist** ❼ (Katedra Św Jana Chrzciciela). Dating from the 13th century, it is the most important building on the island. The interiors feature three chapels of the ambulatory: St Elizabeth's, an example of Italian baroque, the Gothic Marian chapel and the oval Duke's Chapel, an example of Viennese baroque by Fischer von Erlach (1656–1723).

The ★ **National Museum** ❽ (Muzeum Narodowe; open Tues, Wed, Fri, Sun 10am–4pm, Thur 9am–4pm, Sat 10am–6pm) covers the full range of Silesian art, with a fine collection of Gothic wooden sculptures.

A plain, modern, circular building, houses an amazing work of art, the **Racławice Panorama** ❾ (Panorama Racławicka; open Tues–Sun 9am–5pm May–Sept, otherwise 9am–4pm). This view of a battle, painted in Lwów in 1893, depicts the Poles' victorious battle against the Russians in 1794. With a length of 150m (492ft) and a height of 15m (49ft), it is viewed in the round. Paintings of this kind, which were hung in a round building to make them appear three-dimensional, were popular in the 19th century. The Racławice Panorama certainly succeeds, being a stirring evocation of the battle-field.

LEAVING WROCŁAW

The route now leads south through flat countryside to ★ **Świdnica** (pop. 60,000; 360km/225 miles), which has an immense, unmissable building; the Evangelical ★ **Church of Peace**, now the Holy Trinity Church (Kościół Św Trójcy). The half-timbered exterior stems from the devoutly Catholic Habsburg monarchy, which decreed that only wood, clay, sand and straw should be used to build

Star Attraction
● Aula Leopoldina

Trzebnica
Located among the Trzebnickie Hills, about 25km (15½ miles) north of Wrocław, Trzebnica is a centre of the Cult of St Hedwig (Jadwiga), a patron saint of Silesia. Her marble tomb can be seen in the Church of St Bartholomew, which has retained Romanesque and Gothic elements. The church is part of the Cistercian abbey complex, founded in 1202, and is one of Poland's earliest brick buildings.

Tumski Bridge, Wrocław

Map
on pages
66–67

Świdnica

This town, originally an important trading centre linking Germany and Russia, has numerous historic attractions in addition to the Church of Peace. Often referred to as the 'Cracow of Silesia', there are Renaissance and baroque burghers' houses, the Gothic and Renaissance church of Saints Stanisław and Wacław, a baroque town hall, and features such as baroque fountains with statues.

Krzeszów Monastery

Protestant churches. The interiors are a complete contrast, with gleaming, gilded altar, pulpit and organ, and a painted wooden ceiling adds to the splendour. The church can accommodate 7,500 worshippers.

SILESIA'S LARGEST CASTLE

Although **Wałbrzych** (pop.140,000; 383km/239 miles) is essentially an industrial town, there are several places of interest nearby. The most rewarding is ★ **Książ Castle** (open daily 10am–6pm May–Sept, otherwise until 4pm), the largest in Silesia. Constructed in the mid-16th century on the site of a 13th-century fortification, it was rebuilt in the 19th century. The museum's collection comprises ceramics and glass objets d'art.

Another major attraction, 20km (12 miles) from Wałbrzych, is ★★ **Krzeszów Monastery**, Silesia's most important late Baroque ecclesiastic building. Founded by Benedictine monks in the 13th century, it was soon taken over by the Cistercians. It is dominated by the ornate facade of the Church of the Assumption, with its twin towers thought to be the work of Kilian Ignaz Dientzenhofer. The church contains a mausoleum of the Silesian Piast dynasty.

SPA TOWN

Like Krzeszów, **Jelenia Góra** (pop. 95,000; 445km/278 miles) is in a valley ringed by the Sudety Mountains and is a good starting point for excursions. Whitewashed houses with ground-floor arcades line the fine market square, together with the 18th-century town hall, which is the focal point of the Old Town.

The main tourist centre is the historic spa ★**Cieplice Śląskie Zdrój** with hot sulphur springs, now a suburb of Jelenia Góra. The Knights of St John were known to have used the healing properties of the springs to cure skin diseases from 1281. During its heyday in the 18th and 19th centuries, it was a gathering place of the rich and beautiful rather than the infirm.

MOUNTAIN NATIONAL PARK

The German poet Goethe went on excursions to the **Śnieżka** (1,602m/5,255ft), the highest peak in the Karkonosze Mountains; forming part of the Sudety, this is a popular hiking area.

The most beautiful parts of the ★★ **Karkonosze Mountains**, including the Śnieżka, have been established as a **national park** covering an area of 56 sq km (22 sq miles), divided by the Polish/Czech border. Reaching the top of the Śnieżka is no problem, especially since part of the ascent can be made in a chairlift.

At the foot of the Śnieżka is **Karpacz**, a tourist resort which extends uphill with a height difference of 400m (1,300ft) between its various districts.

The district of Bierutowice has a remarkable architectural curiosity: the wooden ★ **Wang Chapel** from the village of Wang in southern Norway. In the 19th century the community was obliged to sell the 13th-century church, which had become too small for the congregation; it was dismantled and eventually arrived at Bierutowice where it was painstakingly reassembled. Although the claim that the two dragons' heads projecting from the gable originally adorned the prows of Viking ships is rather unlikely, their decorative effect is indisputable. Many beams are decorated with mysterious carvings – including winged dragons and double faces.

Star Attractions
- Krzeszów Monastery
- Karkonosze Mountains

Below: Wang Chapel
Bottom: Karkonosze view

Art and Architecture

The typical perception of Poland's architecture is still rooted in the recent Communist past. It's an image of tower blocks and grey urban panoramas. While this element does of course exist, as it does in parts of every European country, this is only one aspect of a vast range of architectural styles.

The Communist regime did not limit construction to purpose-built housing and Modernism. Many historic buildings and entire historic districts of a number of cities were rebuilt and restored from the devastation of World War II. Consequently, in addition to numerous buildings which survived the war intact, there are prime examples of every architectural style, from Romanesque to Gothic, Renaissance, Mannerist, Baroque, rococo, neoclassical, historical revival and Secessionist. There are examples of post-modernism, too. Palaces, castles and country manor houses, cathedrals, churches, abbeys and convents, town halls and burghers' houses reflect all of these styles.

In addition to renowned Polish architects, some of Europe's most celebrated practitioners have left a rich legacy in Poland. Distinguished Italians, such as Santi Gucci, Giovanni Trevano and Bartolomeo Berecci, designed Rennaissance buildings, while some of the most beautiful baroque buildings were the work of the renowned Dutchman, Tylman of Gameren, and the Italian Augustino Locci. The German architect Karl Friedrich Schinkel designed some 19th-century masterpieces.

Museums such as those at Legnica and Biskupin feature some of Poland's earliest important stone and brick buildings, while *skansen* (open-air) museums re-create villages to show historic regional and folk architecture.

Some cities have specific architectural styles. Toruń, for example, has a wealth of Gothic buildings, including a town hall and several churches. Cracow is renowned for its distinguished Rennaissance character, while Sopot has various Secessionist buildings. Only time will tell whether

Opposite: Wawel Cathedral, Cracow
Below: a facade from Wrocław's market square
Bottom: regional architecture, Chochołów

Polish Poster School
While the fine arts were also subject to strict government 'guidelines' and approval, the Polish Poster School flourished from the 1960s, and its main representatives – Jan Lenica, Franciszek Starowieyski, Waldemar Swierzy – transformed the poster from an object designed for a specific commercial or decorative purpose into an art form that could also communicate a powerful political message against the Communist regime.

Warsaw's Palace of Culture

the official Communist style, Socialist Realism, exemplified in Warsaw's Palace of Culture and Science, will ever be prized architecturally.

Along with a variety of architecture comes a variety of art. Considering how many times Poland has been plundered, it is remarkable that museums offer such interesting collections. Paintings by Leonardo da Vinci and Rembrandt can be seen in Cracow's Czartoryski Museum, while Rubens' work hangs in Cracow's Wawel Castle.

Poland has produced outstanding painters of its own, some of whom flourished during the period when Poland was partitioned and, in theory, did not exist. But maintaining and promoting a sense of nationalism played an important role in their works. Jan Matejko (1828–93) is typically cited as Poland's most important painter. Born in Cracow where he worked for most of his life, his main body of work depicts the most important scenes in Polish history on an epic scale and with great emotion. The early 19th-century romantic movement also underlined the country's yearning for independence, depicting numerous rural scenes with a sense of melancholy and aspiration.

The Young Poland (Młoda Polska) movement pioneered Secessionism (central and eastern European Art Nouveau) in Poland, led by celebrated exponents such as Stanisław Wyspiański, while Polish impressionists included Leon Wyczółkowski (1852–1937). The post-war period was dominated by Socialist Realism, the prescribed State style, when posters also emerged as an important art form, and found international favour. It now remains to be seen which artists and styles of art will be championed and appreciated in the democratic era.

Literature, Music and Theatre

For decades Poland was proud of being the country that spent more money per head on culture than anywhere else in the world. This golden age came to a stop with the end of Communism and now all areas of Polish culture, film, theatre, music and literature are largely self-financing and face the commercial realities of a free market economy.

However, Poland's cultural life continues to thrive under democracy, and maintains a highly respected international profile: the guest performances of Polish theatre groups are as enthusiastically applauded as ever, Polish musicians are a permanent fixture at many festivals and the high reputation of the Polish film industry continues. This is undoubtedly due to the deep-seated cultural spirit of the population, the long tradition of culture and its place in the Polish concept of nationhood.

Below: an example of Poland's poster art
Bottom: influential film director Andrzej Wajda (right)

THEATRE AND CINEMA

Polish theatre ranges from a classical repertoire (Mickiewicz, Słowacki, Wyspiański) to modern avant-garde theatre, particularly influenced by Jerzy Grotowski and his Teatr Ubogi (Poor Theatre) in Wrocław, and Tadeusz Kantor of Cracow, who established the popular Cricoteca theatre company.

The Polish film industry had plenty of financial support from the Communists for propaganda films, but some succeeded in establishing a style of their own and indirectly criticising the authorities. Others, such as Roman Polański, who in the 1950s attended the State Film School in Lódż, emigrated in order to have artistic freedom.

LITERATURE

During the partitions of Poland, and the post-war Communist era, many renowned Polish authors and poets saw emigration as their only chance of attaining artistic freedom of expression.

Below: statue of Adam Mickiewicz
Below: music bar on Cracow's Main Market Square

A prime example is the greatest Polish Romantic poet, Adam Mickiewicz (1798–1855), who extolled the aim of regaining independence in his epic poem *Pan Tadeusz* (1834). Like many other Poles active on the cultural scene, Mickiewicz lived in Paris. Similarly, writers such as Joseph Conrad, Witold Gombrowicz, Stanisław Mrozek, Czesław Milosz, Stanisław Lem and Leszek Kolakowski lived and published works beyond their homeland. Their influential, determinedly patriotic opinions were nevertheless heard in Poland; many books were printed for a so-called 'second circulation' illegally, and were thus free from interference by the censors.

MUSIC

The development of Polish music was to a large extent based on patriotic foundations. Chopin, for example, *(see facing page)* used elements of folk music in his compositions, helping to create a climate of nationhood.

Poland's contemporary classical musicians have acquired an international reputation. Witold

Lutosławski and Krzysztof Penderecki, rank among the world's foremost composers. In 1992 music critics discovered the third symphony of a Katowice composer, Henryk Mikołaj Gorecki, written 17 years previously, which became an international phenomenon. Polish jazz musicians such as Tomasz Stanko and Michał Urbaniak, also have reputations beyond Poland's borders.

FREDERIC CHOPIN (1810–49)

Chopin was born in Żelazowa Wola, just outside Warsaw, to a French father and Polish mother. He spent his youth in the capital but also learned all the folk songs and dances of the surrounding villages, which he utilised in almost all his later works. He made his debut as a classical pianist when he was still a young boy, playing in the elegant salons of the aristocracy. His first attempts at composition, mainly polonaises, were also made when he was only a child.

In the autumn of 1830, Chopin left Warsaw, then a small, autonomous duchy, though ultimately under the control of the Russian Tsar, and when the Russians occupied the duchy the following year, Chopin settled in Paris.

In 1836 he met the novelist George Sand who looked after him during his long years of ill health. He travelled with her to Majorca, where he composed his famous *Preludes,* the splendid *Polonaise in A major* and the *Second Sonata in B minor* which includes the funeral march. But his health continued to deteriorate. He returned to France and composed the *Polonaise in A flat major*. In 1847, George Sand left him. Lonely, ill and with little money, he fled to London, where he gave his last public performance. Returning to Paris, he died of tuberculosis in 1849.

Witold Lutosławski
Born in Warsaw in 1913, Witold Lutosławski is one of the great 20th-century composers. His first symphony, written in 1947, was banned by the Stalinist regime, but *Musique Funèbre*, in memory of Bartók, brought him an international reputation in 1958. His last great work was his Symphonie No. 4, commissioned by the Los Angeles Philharmonic Orchestra. He conducted the premier in California in 1993, the year before his death.

Monument at Żelazowa Wola, Chopin's birthplace

Traditions and Customs

Many of Poland's traditions and customs have survived because of their essential role in religious festivals. Christmas is celebrated with a meatless supper comprising 12 courses (one for each apostle) on Christmas Eve. The solemnity of Lent is preceded by *tłusty czwartek* ('fat Thursday') when everyone indulges in eating doughnuts, filled with jam.

On Palm Sunday, palm leaves in churches are used to celebrate Christ's entry into Jerusalem. The most famous Palm Sunday processions take place in Kalwaria Żebrzydowska near Cracow. Various towns also maintain colourful Easter customs, holding a procession of the Guards of the Tomb of Christ.

On Easter Monday a watery awakening is in store. The custom of *Śmigus Dyngus* ranges from gently sprinkling people with perfume, to the more rumbustious practice of throwing buckets of water. The victim is not allowed to retaliate, and the pranks must stop at noon.

The celebrations on Midsummer's Eve (21 June) are rooted in pagan folklore: at night rivers and lakes are transformed by garlands of flowers and burning candles *(wianki)* set afloat on the water. There is a general holiday atmosphere with public festivals, dances, boat parades and fireworks.

All Saints Day at Warsaw's Powązki Cemetery

Festivals

February
Wrocław: 'Musica Polonica Nova', Festival of Contemporary Polish Music.
April
Poznań: Springtime Music.
Częstochowa: Festival of Sacral Music, 'Gaude Mater'.
May
Cracow: International Festival of Short Feature Films.
Wrocław: Festival of Jazz Music 'Jazz on the Odra' (Jazz nad Odrą).
June
Cracow: Cracow Days (Dni Krakowa).
Kazimierz Dolny: Polish Folk Art Fair.
Poznań: International Theatrical Festival.
Stary Sącz: International Festival of Ancient Music.

June–July
Warsaw: Mozart Festival held by the Warsaw Chamber Opera.
June–August
Gdańsk: International Festival of Organ, Choir and Chamber music. 'Musica Sacra'.
July
Zakopane: Karol Szymanowski Music Days.
August
Cracow: 'Music in Old Cracow' Festival.
Duszniki-Zdrój (Lower Silesia): Chopin Festival.
Zakopane: International Festival of Highland Folklore.
Zielona Góra: International Festival of Folk Ensembles.
September
Warsaw: 'Jazz Jamboree' International Festival of Jazz Music.
Warsaw: International Festival of Contemporary Music 'Warsaw Autumn'.
Wrocław: International Oratorio and Cantata Festival 'Wratislavia Cantans'.
October
Warsaw: Chopin International Piano Competition (every five years, next in 2010); Warsaw Film Festival of foreign films.
Wrocław: Open Theatre International Meetings.
December
Cracow: Competition of Cracow Christmas cribs.

Below: celebrating Europe Day in Olsztyn
Bottom: Easter Fair, Cracow

FOOD AND DRINK

Polish food offers a far more comprehensive range than it is given credit for. Among the most popular national dishes are soups and various types of game such as roast duck (usually served with apples), roast venison and *bigos*, a stew which includes sauerkraut, cabbage, and various types of meat.

Barszcz (beetroot soup), *flaki* (tripe soup) and *żurek* (rye soup with sausage) are popular starters. In summer try *chłodnik*, a delicious cold soup made from soured cream, beetroot, cucumber, and hard-boiled egg. Herrings are prepared in various ways (with soured cream is a classic), and salmon and trout are very popular. The delicious *pierogi* are square little pockets of dough stuffed with fillings: curd cheese and mashed potatoes, mince meat, mushrooms, cabbage or fruit. The juicy pork or beef pot roasts are turned into gourmet dishes with the adding of tasty additions and sauces.

Favourite desserts are usually some kind of cake, such as *makowiec* (poppy seed cake), *sernik* (cheesecake), *miodownik* (honey cake), *pierniki* (gingerbread) and *Napoleonki* (mille-feuille).

The Poles are very hospitable and when there are guests for a meal, the table will almost groan under the weight of the wide variety of dishes: 'When a guest is in the home, God is in the home' is an old Polish saying.

In every luxury class hotel you'll find a well-managed restaurant. In addition to national specialities, hotel kitchens also offer a variety of European dishes. In large cities there are numerous restaurants to choose from, offering a wide range of cuisine. This includes the usual burger outlets, inexpensive and gourmet Polish cooking, as well as the pick of the world's more fashionable cuisines, such as French, Italian, Chinese and Japanese.

VODKA

The most popular drink is still vodka (*wódka* in Polish), which literally means 'little water'. The Poles are one of the biggest producers and consumers of vodka in the world.

Although wine is now far more fashionable, being imported means that it is subject to high duty, and the retail price of wine remains higher than vodka.

Since the restructuring of the spirits monopoly Polmos, Polish vodka connoisseurs have been enthralled by the appearance of a host of new names alongside the traditional brands such as Extra Żytnia, and Wyborowa: every distillery can now sell its own range of drinks. As a result there are now estimated to be around 800 vodka brands on the market. Unlike neutral 'international' vodkas which have no flavour, Polish vodkas retain the subtle sweetness and flavour of the rye from which they are distilled. This means they can be sipped and savoured. The country also produces a very good range of lager and mineral

---

Flavoured vodka
Poland produces the largest range of flavoured vodkas, the origins of which are entirely practical. Until the mid-19th century, when the process of purification was developed, vodka was a crude, impure spirit, and adding flavours made it more palatable. This practicality evolved into a speciality, and the range continued to develop during the 19th century.

Opposite: Café Bankowa, Cracow

waters, with blackcurrant juice another speciality.

Restaurant selection

Here are some restaurant suggestions for Poland's most popular destinations, divided into three categories: €€€ (expensive); €€ (moderate); and € (inexpensive):

Warsaw

Belvedere, Stara Pomaranczarnia, Łazienki, tel: 841 4806. An elegant restaurant in an attractive orangery setting in Łazienki Park. €€€

Casa Valdemar, ulica Piękna 7/9, tel: 628 8140. Sophisticated Spanish décor is the setting for a range of Spanish cuisine. €€€

Malinowa, Hotel Bristol, 42/44 Krakowskie Przedmieście, tel: 625 2525. A grand Secessionist setting, with formal and deeply rewarding Polish cuisine. €€€

U Fukiera, Rynek Starego Miasta 27, tel: 831 1013. One of the most popular

> ⚡ **Modern Polish**
> Restaurants have been thriving under privatisation, with one trend being to modernise traditional dishes, while retaining the authentic Polish character.

restaurants in Warsaw; excellent Polish cuisine. €€€

Bazyliszek, Rynek Starego Miasta 1/3, tel: 831 1841. In addition to a splendid view of the Old Town Square, the restaurant also has very good Polish cuisine, specialising in game. €€

Café Blikle, ulica Nowy Świat 33, tel: 826 6619. One of Warsaw's finest and most historic cafés, with a good range of snacks. €

Café Bristol, Hotel Bristol, 42/44 Krakowskie Przedmiescie, tel: 635

8995. Elegant Art Nouveau setting, with superior snacks. €€

Dom Polski, ulica Francuska 11, tel: 616 2432. Delightful 'country villa' setting with a lively garden, and refined Polish cuisine. €€

Restauracja Polska Tradycja, ulica Belwederska 18a, tel: 840 0901. Elegant, traditional town house setting with delicious, sophisticated Polish dishes. €€

Swiętoszek, ulica Jezuicka 6/8, tel: 831 5634. Classic Polish cooking in the Old Town. €€

Podwale, ulica Podwale 25, tel: 635 6314. Traditional Polish food in an attractive Old Town setting with a large al fresco courtyard. €

Cracow

Alef, ulica Szeroka 17, tel: 421 3870. Classic Jewish cuisine in a Bohemian, antique setting in Kazimierz, the historic Jewish district. €€

Amarone, Pod Różą Hotel, ulica Floriańska 14, tel:424 3381. Spacious, attractively modern setting with a great line-up of Italian dishes. €€

Bankowa, Główny Rynek 47, tel: 429 5677. Exquisite café, with only a few tables; beautifully restored. €

Chłopskie Jadło, ulica św Agnieszki 1, tel: 421 8520, also at ulica św Jana 3, tel: 429 5157, ulica Grodzka 9, tel: 429 6187. A 'rustic chic' setting serving classic country dishes with live folk music. €€

Hawelka, Rynek Glowny 34 offers good traditional Polish cuisine. €€

Jama Michalika, ulica Floriańska 45, tel: 422 1561. Flamboyant Secessionist interiors, with a good range of snacks. One of Poland's most famous cafés. €

Metropolitan, ulica Sławkowska 3, tel: 421 9803. Elegant 'retro-chic' setting with a Polish-Euro menu. Stylish and rewarding. €€

Cherubino, ulica św Tomásza 15, tel: 429 4007. Polish and Tuscan cuisine served admid antiques in a traditional country manor house setting. €€

Pod Aniołami, ulica Grodzka 35, tel: 421 3999. Elegantly decorated historic cellar, with regional Polish dishes. €€

Wierzynek, Rynek Glowny 15, tel: 422 1035. The most famous restaurant in Poland: in this house, in 1346, a banquet was held for six emperors and kings plus many dukes and princes. The prices are equally exalted. €€€

Gdańsk

Pod Łososiem, ulica Szeroka 51/54, tel: 301 7652. The most stylish restaurant in town; very popular, so reservation is essential. €€€

Kuchnia Rosyjska,, ulica Długi Targ 11, tel: 301 2735. A themed setting in which various Russian dishes are served. €

Bar Mleczny Neptun, ulica Długa 33–34, tel: 301 2475. A 'no-frills' setting with large portions of various Polish dishes at bargain prices. €

Sopot

Zong Hua, Al Wojska Polskiego, tel: 550 2019. Chinese cuisine in a charming seaside villa. €€

Malbork

Zamkowa, ulica Staroscinska 14, tel: 272736. Located near the castle. Good Polish cooking. €€€

Poznań

Bażanciarnia, Stary Rynek 94, tel: 855 3358. Distinguished Polish cuisine in a sophisticated town house setting that's been beautifully decorated, and overlooks the market square. €€–€€€

Toruń

Karczma u Damroki, Al Solidarnośći 1, tel: 622 3660. Polish and European dishes served in a 'rustic chic' wooden farmhouse, on the edge of the *skansen* museum. €€

Pod Modrym Fartuchem, Rynek Nowomiejski , tel: 622 2626. Established in 1489, charming café with a good range of Polish snacks. €

Kuranty, ulica Rynek Staromiejski 29, tel: 662 5252. Overlooking the market square, a 1920s decor is an ideal setting for Polish and European cuisine. €

Staropolski, Zeglarska 10/14, tel: 622 6061, fax: 626 5384. Good Polish cuisine, in the same building as the Staropolska Hotel. €

Zamość

Hetmanska, ulica Staszica 7. Good house specialities. €€€

Café in the Market Square, Poznań

ACTIVE PURSUITS

WATER SPORTS

Poland offers a wide range of sports facilities. The Baltic coast and numerous lakes are ideal for water sport fans in particular. There are lots of beaches suitable for bathing along the Baltic Coast.

Those who prefer to swim or sail in fresh water have the thousand lakes of Masuria and the Pomeranian lake district to choose from. Windsurfing has also become increasingly popular. On the Masurian lakes windsurfers are still rather exotic and are obliged to share the water with canoeists.

The many lakes in idyllic settings are often linked by rivers and canals, so that canoe tours of several days' duration can be planned. This is also facilitated by the fact that the most attractive lake shores have bivouac places for overnight stops in the midst of nature. The most beautiful river to canoe on is the 200-km (124-mile) Krutynia route, which winds its way through glorious countryside. The river is well supplied with bars, canteens, landing stages and bivouac grounds, and water sports equipment

is available to rent. Information: Polish Kayaking Union: Polski Zwiazek Kajakowy, ulica Erazma Ciołka 17, 01445 Warsaw, tel: 022-837 4059, www.pzkaj.pl.

FISHING

The angling season in Poland lasts all year round and the abundant supply of fish in the rivers is attracting increasing numbers of anglers. Brown and rainbow trout are plentiful in the mountain rivers of Pomerania and the Masurian Lake District is a paradise for flyfishers. The trout fishing season is, however, closed in winter months, and there are sometimes limits on catches of trout and other fish.

In the Masurian lakes fishing with bait is allowed only for catching pike, perch and catfish. The fighting barbels can be fished in the lower courses of the Pomeranian Mountains, while they abound in the fast waters of southern Poland.

Many angling shops offer equipment at low prices but visitors need a licence to fish. Ask at the tourist office for details *(see page 120)*.

During the summer season boat companies in the coastal resorts offer

Skiing in the Tatras

deep-sea fishing excursions. The Polish Angling Union (Polski Związek Węgkarski, www.zgpzw.pl) is at ulica Twarda 42, tel: 620 5085. It has branches all over the country.

CYCLING

Poland is an ideal country for cyclists. Masuria is a popular destination, even though some of it is hilly, and the coastal region is also suitable for cycle tours. Quiet side roads, which are usually asphalted, are perfect for cyclists, but main roads should be avoided; there are no cycle paths in Poland.

HORSE RIDING

Horses are well respected in Poland, which has a great cavalry tradition, and horses still work on the land. Arab breeding, which was internationally renowned between the two world wars, remains an important export industry. There are numerous riding centres and state as well as privately-owned stud farms offering 'holidays in the saddle', with possibilities ranging from a day's riding to longer stays with accommodation. Riding lessons are also available and this is a good place to learn to ride.

There are equestrian centres such as Łąck, northwest of Warsaw, which also offers lessons in driving horse-drawn carriages. Racut, in the Poznań region, offers accommodation in a grand neo-classical palace, formerly owned by the Dutch king Wihelm I. Kadyny, close to the Baltic coast near Gdańsk and Elbląg, has an important stud farm, with accommodation available in the Kadyny Hotel, which incorporates the former summer residence of Emperor Wilhelm II of Germany. The addresses of these and other centres can be obtained from the Polish Equestrian Sports Association: Polski Związek Jezdziecki, Lekty Karska 29, 01687 Warsaw, tel: 022-639 3240, www.pzj.pl

CLIMBING

The Sudety Mountains and the Carpathians provide many opportunities for mountain climbing. In the Tatra Mountains there are numerous climbing routes, involving a combination of mountain hiking and actual climbing. In recent years a well-sign-posted network of trails has also been laid out in the Sudety. In the Tatra Mountains climbers who do not know the area should not embark on proper climbing tours without a guide.

SKIING

In winter the Tatra Mountains, which have an alpine character, have plenty to offer skiing enthusiasts, whether downhill or cross-country, and they are covered with snow from December through to March; in the highest areas, the snow remains until May. The winter sports mecca is Zakopane, which calls itself Poland's Winter Capital.

The Sudety Mountains have idyllic winter sports resorts, and Szczyrk in the Silesian Beskid Mountains are also very attractive. The cross-country tracks in the Olsztyn area are now well-known, especially as snow is guaranteed in the winter months. There is also snow in Masuria, offering good cross-country skiing.

For further details of nature and activity holidays in Poland, visit www.poland.com

---

Hiking

If you enjoy hiking then a journey to Poland offers various marked trails in different parts of the country, and through different types of countryside, such as hills, mountains, valleys, national parks and lake districts. In areas such as the Tatra Mountains, part of the Tatra National Park, hikes can only be undertaken by following marked trails.

PRACTICAL INFORMATION

Getting There

BY AIR

Most international flights land at Warsaw, where a new terminal was opened in 1992 to handle the increasing number of passengers both with LOT, the Polish airline, and British Airways. Scheduled flights are codeshared between the two airlines, as well as various other international carriers. There are regular non-stop flights from London, New York, Chicago and Montreal. LOT also has a codeshare agreement with American Airlines. The flight time from the UK to Poland is around 2½ hours. International flights can also land at Cracow, Gdańsk, Katowice, Poznan, Rzeszów and Szczecin.

In the UK: LOT Polish Airlines, 414 Chiswick High Road, London W4 5TF, tel: 0845-6010949; www.lot.com

In the US: LOT Polish Airlines, 500 Fifth Avenue, Suite 408, New York NY 10036, tel: 1-718 6562632.

Additionally, low-cost carriers include Ryanair, Easyjet and Wizzair, offering flights from Luton and Stansted Airport to Warsaw, Gdańsk, Poznan, Katowice and Wrocław. Routes also operate to Poland and other European cities. Log onto www.ryanair.com; www.easyjet.com; www.wizzair.com

---

LOT services
LOT also offers domestic flights linking various Polish cities from, or via, Warsaw Airport. This includes Bydgoszcz, Gdańsk, Katowice, Kołobrzeg, Koszalin, Cracow, Łódz, Poznań, Rzeszów, Szczecin, Wrocław and Zielona Góra. LOT also operates services between Warsaw and various other Central and Eastern European cities, including Berlin, Budapest, Lvov, Moscow and St Petersburg.

BY RAIL

There are international rail links between Poland and neighbouring European countries; from London a daily service runs from Waterloo and goes via Brussels, with a change in Cologne.

In the UK: International Rail Centre, Victoria Station, London SW1, tel: 08705 848848 or book on-line at www.raileurope.co.uk

In the US: Raileurope Inc., toll free on 1-800-4-EURAIL.

BY COACH

Inexpensive coach services to Poland are becoming an increasingly popular alternative to the train travel. Weekly services are run in luxury, air-conditioned coaches. There are buses from London Victoria Coach Station via Poznań, Konin, Łódz and Warsaw; or from London or Manchester/Birmingham to Wrocław, Katowice and Cracow. The journey from London to Warsaw takes about 26 hours. Contact Polorbis, tel: 020-8748 3062.

BY CAR

From the Hook of Holland or Ostend on the Dutch coast, the driving time to the Polish border is about 12 hours. Motorists should be in possession of an international driving licence, car registration documents, fully comprehensive international insurance, and Green Card.

Getting Around

BY AIR

LOT, the Polish national airline operates routes to 12 cities and towns throughout Poland. Book through LOT offices or Orbis travel agents.

BY BUS

A well-developed network of bus routes links Polish cities. All the larger towns have good public transport systems, consisting of trams, buses and trolleybuses, and it is possible to reach many tourist attractions in this way. Tickets can be bought at newsagent kiosks (Kiosk Ruch), some shops and sometimes from the bus driver. A separate ticket is required with every transfer, and tickets must 'stamped' by onboard ticket machines. One-day and weekly passes are also available. From 11pm the night rates come into force, which is more than the usual fare.

BY RAIL

A Polrail Pass entitles you to unlimited use of all Polish trains within a certain period with no limit to the distance travelled. This can be obtained in Poland or in Britain through the International Rail Centre *(see opposite)*. Train timetables can be viewed on the Polish State Railways website, www.pkp.com.pl

BY CAR

Leaded and unleaded petrol is available throughout the country. The speed limit in built-up areas is 50 kph (31 mph), outside built-up areas 90 kph (56 mph); on motorways it is 130 kph (68 mph). Seat belts are mandatory in front and back seats. From October 1– March 1 dipped headlights must be used in daytime. Cars on roundabouts have right of way, so do all trams. A green arrow at traffic lights indicates that right turns are permitted even when the lights are red.

CAR HIRE

The major car hire firms such as Hertz, Avis, Budget and National Car Rental operate from airport, hotel and city locations. To hire a car, you must be at least 21, be in possession of a valid passport, visa (if necessary) and international driver's licence.

Security precautions
As when travelling anywhere in the world, make sure you keep your luggage with you at all times, and take sensible precautions, particularly when travelling at night.

HITCH-HIKING

This is allowed as long as you buy a hitch-hikers book with 2,000km-worth of coupons. These are available from 'IT' tourist information centres and branches of the Polish Society of Youth Hostels (PTSM). The hitch-hiking season runs from May to September.

Facts for the Visitor

TRAVEL DOCUMENTS

British visitors can stay for six months without a visa (your passport must be valid for at least 6 months after your date of departure). Passport holders from most European countries, the US and the Commonwealth can stay for up to 90 days without a visa. Visitors are obliged to register their stay within 48 hours after crossing the border, which can be done at the hotel or campsite where you are staying.

Foreign visitors who wish to stay more than 90 days should report to the registration office in the nearest major town for a visa or extension of one.

Loss or theft of a passport should be reported at once to the consulate of the country that issued it in order to receive a substitute travel document.

TOURIST INFORMATION

Most towns and cities will have one of the numerous tourist information offices displaying the 'IT' logo. They are usually run by the local Orbis offices and the Polish Tourist Association (PTTK). There are also IT desks in large hotels providing comprehensive information for visitors. To obtain information about Poland before you set out, contact either Orbis (Polorbis) or the Polish National Tourist Office:

In the UK: Polish National Tourist Office, e-mail: info@visitpoland.org; www.visitpoland.org Polorbis (tour operator), 1st Floor, 234 King St, London W6 ORF, tel: 020 8748 3062.

In the US: Polish National Tourist Office, 275 Madisson Ave, Suite 1711, New York, NY 10016, tel: 212-338 9412; e-mail: pntonyc@polandtour.org; www.polandtour.org Orbis (tour operator), 500 Fifth Ave, Suite 1428, New York, NY 10036, tel: 212-391 0844.

In Poland: Warsaw, branches at Pl. Zamkowy 1/13, Krakowskie Przedmieście 39; Main Hall of the Central Railway Station, and Arrivals Hall, International Terminal of Fryderyk Chopin Airport; tel: 022-9431; www.warsaw tour.pl **Cracow**, Rynek Główny (Main Market Sq) 1–3 Sukiennice, tel: 012-421 7706, www.mcit.pl; **Toruń**, Rynek Staromiejski 25, tel: 056-621 0931, www.it.torun.pl **Opole**, ulica Krakowska 15, tel: 077-451 1987, www.opole.pl; **Częstochowa**, al Najświętszej Marii Panny 65, tel: 034-368 2250, www.czestochowa.pl; **Gdańsk**, ulica Długa 45, tel: 058-301 6096/301

A new shopping centre, Szczecin

1343, www.pttk-gdansk.pl; **Szczecin**, Zamek, ulica Korsarzy 34, tel: 091-489 1630, www.zamek.szczecin.pl; **Zakopane**, ulica Kościuszki 17, tel: 018-201 2211, www.zakopane.pl; **Wrocław**, Rynek 14, tel: 071-344 3111, www.wroclaw.div.pl; **Poznań**, Stary Rynek 59–60, tel: 061-852 6156, www.cim.poznan.pl

CURRENCY AND EXCHANGE

The Polish unit of currency is the złoty, divided into 100 groszy. In circulation are coins to the value of 1, 2, 5, 10, 20, and 50 groszy and 1, 2, and 5 złoty; złoty notes are in denominations of 10, 20, 50, 100, and 200.

As well as banks there are numerous private exchange offices *(kantor)*. Rates can vary significantly between offices. Traveller's cheques can be difficult to exchange and it may be necessary to go to a bank. Most convenient are the ATMs now found in many places.

There is no black market in Poland and if you are offered currency exchange rate on the street, don't accept it – the notes are almost bound to be counterfeit.

Credit cards are accepted by ever-more establishments, and this is now standard practice among hotels, airline companies, car hire firms, travel agents, restaurants and, increasingly, shops.

CUSTOMS

All foreign currencies may be imported and exported without restriction. Tourists are in theory obliged to declare the value of their currency when entering or leaving the country, by filling out forms given by passport control officers.

There is no restriction on bringing items for personal use or presents, so long as the quantity does not suggest that the intention is to sell them. EU regulations apply to Polish goods taken out of the country. Customs regulations can be viewed at www.clo.gov.pl

Car drivers can take out only 10 additional litres of petrol in their reserve can in addition to what they have in the tank.

TIPPING

The price in restaurants usually includes a service charge. Here, however, as in all other relevant branches of the economy, such as taxis and hairdressers, tips at 10 percent are gladly received as a token of appreciation of good service.

OPENING TIMES

The opening times of shops, offices and museums vary considerably and museums and other tourist attractions are prone to change. Most businesses open weekdays 8am–5pm and close on Sundays.

Shops: In general it may be said that the larger the place, the more convenient the hours are for customers. Thus in every large town there is at least one grocery store open round the clock. Usually, in the towns, shops are open on weekdays 6am to 6 or 7pm and Sat 7am–1pm, closed Sun and holidays. In the country shops may close at 5pm, and markets run from 7am–7pm.

Banks: The private exchange offices are generally open from 8am until 6

> **All-day dining**
> Most restaurants serve food throughout the day without any breaks, so a very late lunch is no problem. City centre restaurants often state their closing time as 'when the last guest leaves'.

or 7pm and bank exchange counters usually stay open until 5pm.

Post Offices: Outside large towns post offices open from 8am–8pm. In cities one main branch is open 24 hours.

Restaurants: Those listed in *Food and Drink* usually open at noon and close at around 10pm or, in city centre locations, midnight.

Museums: Museums usually close on Mondays. From October to the end of April, they generally close earlier in the day. It is best to ask about opening hours beforehand at a tourist information office ('IT'), whose own hours vary, but they are generally open daily during the tourist season.

PUBLIC HOLIDAYS

In addition to 3 May (Constitution Day in honour of the Constitution of 1791), the public holidays are New Year's Day, Easter Monday, Labour Day (1 May), Corpus Christi, Assumption Day (15 Aug), All Saints' Day (1 Nov) and the two days at Christmas (25 and 26 Dec). Good Friday and Whit Monday are not official public holidays.

The 22 July holiday marking the founding of Communist Poland was dropped and replaced by National Independence Day on 11 November, marking the resurrection of the Polish State in November 1918.

POSTAL SERVICES

Letterboxes are usually red; the green boxes are for local letters only and the blue for airmail letters. Stamps are sold at post offices, which are usually open from 8am to 8pm, and also at many IT kiosks and hotels where postcards are also sold. The price of stamps for letters and cards abroad may be subject to change: ask at the post office or hotel reception what the current rates are.

TELEPHONE

Most public telephone boxes now have card phones, only some still require special tokens *(żetony)*. In contrast to the token-operated telephones, which can only be used to make local or national calls, the new card telephones are easy to use. Telephone cards can be bought in different denominations from post offices, and these phones can be used to make international calls. There are still places which do not have direct dialling facilities, where the call has to be placed through the operator (code for the UK: 0044, for the US: 001). It is sometimes difficult to get a line to Poland from another country (code for Poland: 48). If phoning from outside Warsaw, first dial zero and wait for the second tone. AT&T: 010 480 0111; MCI: 010 480 0222; Sprint: 00 800 111 3115.

NEWSPAPERS AND RADIO

The Times, *International Herald Tribune, Time* and *Newsweek* can be obtained in major cities on newsstands, in hotels and some grocery stores, usually one day after publication. *Warsaw Voice*, a publication in English, is available not just in the capital but also in major tourist centres. This is aimed particularly at foreign visitors and includes numerous events listings and up-to-date tourist tips. For those with an interest in politics, there is a publication of news articles translated into English called *Inside*. Free tourist publications, such as *Welcome to Warsaw*, are available in various cities. Inexpensive city listings magazines such as *Kraków In Your Pocket* are available at newsstands and tourist offices.

The established radio stations follow the old Eastern European tradition and broadcast outside the Western European frequency range of 66–73 MHz. Conversion to Western European standards have also become established, with a greater range of English-language programmes.

SECURITY

The dramatic economic and social changes following the democratic elections have been accompanied by an increase in crime since the early 1990s. As usual, when travelling anywhere, it is vital to take sensible safety precautions, especially in the big cities. This applies particularly to motorists, whose deluxe Western vehicles are coveted by the criminal element. The chances of getting your car back are small, and stolen property generally disappears for good across Poland's eastern borders. Always

---

Souvenirs

The choice of souvenirs to take home from Poland will depend primarily on the region in which you spend your holiday. On the Baltic coast, for example, by far the most popular souvenir is amber, either in its natural state or as jewellery, while in the Karkonosze it is lead crystal. Modern art or examples of traditional handicrafts (wood carvings, embroidered mats, pottery) also make an attractive present or memento. Good quality craft articles are available from the Cepelia shops (e.g. in Old Town Market Square in Warsaw).

When buying at markets it is always a good idea to compare prices and to bargain. Collectors of nostalgic or unusual items can still find bargains at the numerous flea markets. However, no articles which were produced before 1945 can be taken out of the country without the permission of the local conservator's office.

make sure that your car is left in supervised car parks and ensure that you have adequate insurance for luggage and cash as well.

TIME

Central European Time, an hour ahead of Greenwich Mean Time, is used across the country. Daylight saving time applies from May to September when the clocks move forward an hour.

VOLTAGE

Electricity is 220V. Round two-pin plugs are used. Remember to take an adaptor.

INTERNET

The phone number 0 202122 provides an internet link anywhere in Poland

MEDICAL

Visitors can get medical attention in any city clinic. Medicines and drugs prescribed by doctors may be paid for in złotys. A comprehensive travel insurance policy or a private health insurance policy taken out before you travel is strongly recommended.

There is a good range of basic, inexpensive medicines available from pharmacies, but most special medication is not stocked and has to be ordered, which takes time. It is therefore essential to take with you any medication on which you are reliant. If you are planning to spend time in country areas, particularly close to the eastern border, it is advisable to see your doctor about the symptoms and treatment of Lyme disease before travelling.

Pharmacies are open during normal business hours. The addresses of the closest chemists on night duty are posted in the window.

EMERGENCIES

Ambulance: tel: 999
Police: tel: 997 or 112 if calling from a mobile, for foreigners 0800 200 300
Fire: tel: 998

PHOTOGRAPHY

Well-known brands of films and photographic material are readily available at prices comparable to those in the West. Larger towns have photo laboratories which can process your holiday photos in an hour.

DIPLOMATIC REPRESENTATION

United Kingdom Embassy: aleja Róz 1, Warsaw, tel: 022-311 00 00.
UK Consulate: ulica św Anny 9, Cracow, tel: 421 7030.

Hand in hand in Cracow

ACCOMMODATION

A wide range of accommodation is available for visitors to Poland, from luxury international standard hotels to comfortable tourist-class hotels, guesthouses, rooms in private houses and camp sites in beautiful, remote areas.

HOTELS

Luxury hotels provide Western standards at corresponding prices and belong to international hotel chains such as Inter-continental and Marriott. Many hotels operated by Poland's former state monopoly, Orbis, have been privatised and modernised with foreign capital, while others are still waiting for the necessary renovation. The prices of an overnight stay vary considerably and also differ according to the season and length of stay. The system of grading hotels on the basis of a star rating can also be misleading, as some luxury hotels have voluntarily 'downgraded' their star ranking in response to the graduated value-added tax which was introduced in 1994. The level of this tax depends on the 'degree of luxury' of the goods and services, ranging anywhere from 0 percent up to 25 percent.

The Grand Hotel, Sopot

Inns and motels can be found along principal main roads and many of them have a regional flavour. A 'pensjonat' is the equivalent to the British B&B and located in popular tourist spots. Rooms in private homes can also be reserved through local tourist agencies. Small, privately-run boarding houses have also become established in popular tourist spots. They are recommended for a real flavour of Polish hospitality and can also be reserved through tourist agencies, which can also advise on rooms in private houses.

Hotel selection

The following are suggestions for Poland's main cities, listed according to the following categories: €€€ (expensive); €€ (moderate); € (inexpensive).

Cracow (area code 012)

Hotel Copernicus, ulica Kanonicza 16, tel: 424 3400, fax: 424 3405; www.hotel.com.pl Attractive and modern interiors behind a period facade. €€€
Elektor Hotel, ulica Szpitalna 28, tel: 423 2317, fax: 423 2327; www.hotelelektor.com.pl Historic, central hotel. €€€

Francuski, ulica Pijarska 13, tel: 422 5122, fax: 422 5270; email: www.orbis.pl A traditional hotel restored to all its former glory. €€€

Grand, ulica Sławkowska 5/7, tel: 421 7255, fax: 421 8360; www.grand.pl One of Cracow's most traditional hotels, with Secessionist decor. €€€

Hotel pod Różą, ulica Floriańska 14, tel: 422 3300, fax: 421 43351, www. hotel.com.pl. Charming, friendly and located near the market square. €€€

Demel, ulica Głowackiego 22, tel: 636 1600, fax: 636 4543, www.demel.. com.pl.. Very friendly service. €€

Hotel Ester, ulica Szeroka 20, tel: 429 1188, fax: 429 1233, www.hotel-ester. krakow.pl. In the centre of the Kazimierz district, this hotel has recently been created in an attractive manner. €€

Klezmer-Hois, ulica Szeroka 6, tel/ fax: 411 1245; www.klezmer.pl Original 1930s' decor in a perfect location in the Kazimierz district. €€

Hotel Royal, ulica św Gertrudy 26–29, tel: 421 3500, fax 425 5857; www.royal.com.pl Overlooking the Wawel Castle, in the Planty gardens, the hotel is late 19th century. €€

Hotel Wit Stwosz, ulica Mikołajska 28, tel: 429 6026, fax: 429 6139, www.wit-stwosz.com. A period building in the Old Town. €

Hotel Wyspiański, ulica Westerplatte 15, tel: 422 9566, fax: 422 5719; www. hotel-wyspianski.pl. Former hostel, upgraded to provide range of accommodation. €

Gdańsk (area code 058)

Hotel Hanza, ulica Tokarska 6, tel: 305 3427, fax: 305 3386; www.hanza-hotel.com.pl Modern luxurious hotel in the heart of the old town. €€€

Hevelius, ulica Heweliusza 22, tel: 321 0000, fax: 321 0020; www.orbis.pl. Modern, welcoming, comfortable hotel a few minutes walk from the Old Town. €€€

Novotel Gdańsk Marina, ulica Jelitkowska 20, tel: 553 0100, fax: 553

> **Planning accommodation**
> The tourist information centres in Warsaw, including the central railway station and Krakowskie Przedmiescie 39, tel: 9431, can advise on hotels and make reservations for you in Warsaw.

0460; www.orbis.pl.A modern, coastal hotel with a pool, close to Sopot. €€€

Hotel Podewils, ul Szafarnia 2, tel: 300 9560, fax:300 9570, www.podewils-hotel.pl. A waterside setting in the historic centre, furnished with antiques. €€€

Novotel, ulica Pszenna 1, tel: 300 2750, fax: 300 2950; www.orbis.pl Modern, comfortable low-rise, just across the Motława Canal from the Old Town. €€

Poznań (area code 061)

Hotel Royal, ul Św Marian 71, tel: 858 2300, fax: 853 7884, www.hotel-royal.com.pl. Located on the principal shopping street, near the old town, the hotel occupies a pair of period town-houses. €€

Brovaria, Stary Rynek 73–74, tel: 858 6868, fax: 858 6869, www.brovaria.pl. Stylish modernity within a historic building overlooking the market square. €€

Sopot (area code 058)

Hotel Grand, ulica Powstańców Warszawy 12, tel: 551 0041, fax: 551 6124; www.orbis.pl Art Nouveau hotel overlooking the beach, with fine sea views. €€€

Hotel Haffner, ul JJ Haffnera 59, tel: 550 9999, fax: 550 9800, www.hotel-haffner.pl. Stylish hotel, centrally located with a pool, fitness centre and spa. €€€

Pensjonat Eden, ulica Kordeckiego 4/6, tel/fax: 551 1503. Historic, attractive seaside villa, in a pleasant park. €

Szczecin (area code 091)

Neptun, ulica Matejki 18, tel: 488 3883, fax: 488 4117; email: neptun@

orbis.pl Has all the comforts of a first-class hotel you'd expect. €€€

Radisson, plac Rodła 10, tel: 359 5595, fax: 359 4594; www.radissonsas.com.pl The best and most modern hotel in the city. €€€

Warsaw (area code 022)

Bristol, ulica Krakowskie Przedmieście 42/44, tel: 551 1000, fax: 625 2577; www.lemeridien-bristol.com Beautiful Secessionist hotel, with swimming pool and renowned restaurant. €€€

Holiday Inn, ulica Złota 48–54, tel: 697 3999, fax: 697 3899; email: holiday@orbis.pl Modern low rise by the central railway station and Palace of Culture. €€€

Marriott, aleja Jerozolimskie 65/79, tel: 630 6306, fax: 630 5239; www.marriott.com/wawpl Modern, deluxe skyscraper offering great views, with facilities including a swimming pool and numerous restaurants. €€€

Polonia Palace Hotel, al Jerozolimskie 45, tel: 318 2800, fax: 318 2801, www.poloniapalace.com. Beautifully restored, luxurious hotel dating from 1913, by the main shopping area. €€€

Victoria Sofitel, ulica Krolewska 11, tel: 657 8011, fax: 657 8057; www.orbis.pl Well-appointed modern low-rise, with a swimming pool, overlooking the Saxon Gardens, close to the Old Town. €€€

Hotel Rialto, ulica Wilcza 73, tel: 584 8700, fax: 584 8701; www.hotelrialto.com.pl 'Boutique' hotel with an elegant Art Deco style and superb restaurant. €€€

Le Regina, ulica Koscielna 12, tel: 531 6000, fax: 531 6001; www.leregina.com. Beautifully restored 18th-century palace, with swimming pool and courtyard garden, on the edge of the Old Town district. €€€

Harenda, ulica Krakowskie Przedmieście 4/6, tel: 826 0071, fax: 826 2625; www.hotelharenda.com.pl Inexpensive, practical and central option. €

Wrocław (area code 071)

Wrocław, ulica Powstańców Śląskich 5–7, tel: 361 4651, fax: 361 6617, www.orbis.pl. In the city centre; has a swimming pool, sauna and solarium and facilities for disabled guests. €€€

Hotel HP Park Plaza, ulica Drobnera 11–13, tel: 320 8400, fax: 320 8445; www.parkplaza.pl New, modern hotel with a central location and a fitness centre. €€

Zakopane (area code 018)

Litwor Hotel, ulica Krupówki 40, tel: 202 4200, fax: 202 4205, www.litwor.pl. In a perfect central location, this is a stylish and well-appointed venue; a great restaurant, pool and fitness centre. €€

CAMPING AND AGROTOURISM

Poland is a paradise for campers, with hundreds of camp sites for overnight stays in the midst of nature. Camp sites are graded in three categories and are usually open 15 May–15 Sept. Many have simply-furnished chalets, too. For reservations, contact the Polish Caravan and Camping Association (Polska Federacja Campingu i Carawaningu), ulica Grochowska 331, Warsaw 03-823, tel: 810 60 50, www.pfcc.info. For agrotourist holidays contact Gospodarstwa Gościnne, Polish Federation of Rural Tourism, ulica Wspólna 30, Warsaw 00-930, tel: 602 305 330, www.agritourism.pl.

Hostels

In addition to the youth hostels, which are open all year round, there are also seasonal youth hostels open just in the summer. An international youth hostel card entitles you to a 25 percent reduction. Although the hostels are in principle open to all age groups, preference is given to those under 26. Book four weeks in advance. Polish Youth Hostels Association (PTSM), at ulica Chocimska 14, 00 791 Warsaw, tel: 849 8128, www.ptsm.org.pl.

INDEX